AIR FORCE ONE

An Honor, Privilege,
and Pleasure to Serve

To Russ Thompson
with Best Wishes

John L. Haugh Sr

Printed in the United States of America.

ISBN: 978-1-59571-888-4
Library of Congress Control Number: 2013905209

Designed and published by

Word Association Publishers
205 Fifth Avenue
Tarentum, Pennsylvania 15084

www.wordassociation.com
1.800.827.7903

AIR FORCE ONE

An Honor, Privilege, and Pleasure to Serve

John L. Haigh Sr.

Chief Master Sergeant (Ret).
United States Air Force
Former Chief Steward: Air Force One

WORD ASSOCIATION PUBLISHERS
www.wordassociation.com
1.800.827.7903

DEDICATION

To Mother and Father, Sam and Kathryn Haigh;
my sisters, Leola and Kathryn;
my brothers, Sam, Tom, and Ben;
my wife, Phyllis (deceased).

To Susan, Gene, John Jr., Wallace, Xarissa, Linda, Marilyn, Don,
Dwaine, Tommy, and Joanne.

To my wife, Jessie.

To Dawn, Julie, and TJ.

To the crew of Air Force One and Special Air Missions,
home of Air Force One, Andrews Air Force Base, Maryland.

ODE TO AIR FORCE ONE

BY JOHN L. HAIGH, SR.

Air Force One
Is the silver winged symbol
of the free world
carrying its most powerful leaders
to all points of the globe
at a moment's notice
never conceding,
never retreating,
and always on alert
to defeat the enemies of freedom

CONTENTS

Chapter 1: Special Air Missions (1973 – 1979)

Chapter 2: In Service to President Jimmy Carter (Sept. 1, 1979 – Jan. 20, 1981)

Chapter 3: In Service to President Ronald Reagan (Jan. 20, 1981 – Jan. 20, 1989)

Chapter 4: In Service to President George H. W. Bush (Jan. 20, 1989 – June 30, 1992)

Chapter 5: Life After Air Force One

Author's Note: *While it's typical to italicize the names of aircraft, ships, etc., I have purposely chosen to leave the "Air Force One" call sign in standard font because it appears so many times and might be less reader-friendly otherwise. All other such names are italicized per usual style guidelines.*

Thank you for your understanding.

CHAPTER 1

SPECIAL AIR MISSIONS
(1973 – 1979) ///

MY GOAL TO TRAVEL and see the world started in March 1963 at McGuire Air Force Base, New Jersey. Little did I know that ten years later, I would volunteer and be accepted into the 89th Military Airlift Wing, Special Air Missions Organization, at Andrews Air Force Base, Maryland—home of Air Force One. And that is where my story begins …

Apollo 17 Astronauts

In July 1973, I was selected to be part of the crew transporting the *Apollo 17* astronauts, along with their wives and staff, on a presidential goodwill trip around the world, hosted by the heads of state at each stop. Due to the nature of the mission, a top-secret clearance was required of all personnel, so I gained the clearance and got the green light.

We served the astronauts—Navy Captains Gene Cernan and Ron Evans—and civilian geologist Dr. Harrison Schmitt. We traveled to

PRIME CREW OF ELEVENTH MANNED APOLLO MISSION
Harrison H. Schmitt   Ronald E. Evans   Eugene A. Cernan

Spain, the Canary Islands, Africa (with seven stops there), Pakistan, India, Singapore, Indonesia, the Philippines, Guam, the Marshall Islands, and Honolulu in Hawaii, and then we returned to Andrews Air Force Base.

While I have some good memories of that trip, Honolulu in particular comes to mind, and not just because it was so beautiful. Captain Cernan, the lead astronaut, and his wife had invited the flight crew to their personal suite on the twenty-fifth floor of the Hyatt Regency Hotel, overlooking Waikiki Beach. He'd said that we had taken such good care of them for the past month, they would like to be our hosts for a change.

So there I was, standing out on the balcony and talking to Captain Cernan. A full moon hung overhead, and at one point, Captain Cernan looked up at it.

"You know," he said, "when I was a young boy, I often wondered what it would be like to walk on the moon. And now that I've been there and done that, I know!"

I got goose bumps all over. That was indeed a moment to remember!

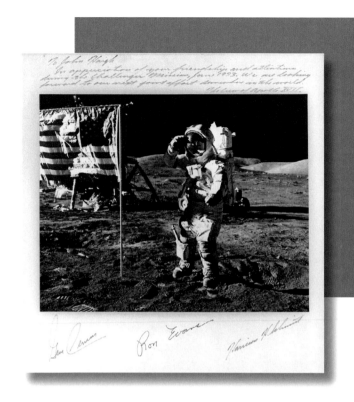

Secretary of State Kissinger

A fellow steward and I were on a mission carrying US secretary of state Dr. Henry Kissinger to Mexico City. My colleague had flown with the secretary on previous missions, and thus he had been assigned to serve him on this trip. The secretary came aboard and went directly to the state room compartment. The other steward walked in behind him to present the itinerary and menu of the day. A moment later, he came out of the state room, looking red faced and saying, "Henry's hot! He chewed me out." I laughed of course!

The flight was five hours long, and Dr. Kissinger did not see or talk to me the entire trip. Upon landing in Mexico City, the other steward and I positioned ourselves a few steps forward of the state room door. As the secretary was departing, he walked past the other steward without saying a word to him. He stopped in front of me, reached out and grasped my hand, then said, "Vunderful job, Sergeant," and then he deplaned. The other steward stood there, dumfounded.

That was nothing, though! Five days later, we were returning to Washington with Dr. Kissinger. The secretary once again did not see or talk to me during the five-hour flight. After landing and taxiing to the arrival spot, the other steward stood alone just forward of the state room door, and I was at my position in the front galley. The secretary emerged from the state room, walked past the other steward without saying a word, and then stopped at the front galley. He reached toward me, grasped my hand, looked me in the eye, and said, "Vunderful job, Sergeant," and then he deplaned. I looked over at the other steward, who had a "What am I? Chopped liver?" look on his face.

"It must be my good looks," I said.

Secretary of Defense Schlesinger

A funny, but humbling, moment occurred on a return trip from London while carrying the secretary of defense, James Schlesinger. I was cooking, and my fellow steward was serving the secretary. We had served the entire official party and flight crew, but when it came time to serve Secretary Schlesinger, we were delayed by several press conferences. Meanwhile, his breakfast was on hold in the oven. The biscuits being served were the old-fashioned type—like Grandma used to make, as they say. There was only one catch: after heating them for the third time, they got harder than a brick bat. We finally served him, and when he tried to eat the biscuit, it crumbled in his hand. He looked at the steward and said, "Can't you do any better than this?"

The steward said, "TOAST!"

It was then fifteen minutes from arrival at Andrews Air Force Base. The steward came to me and said, "The man wants toast." I had just cleaned up the galley and secured everything for landing. But I replied fervently: "TOAST!"

I made the toast, and the steward said, "BUTTER IT!"

> "Can't you do any better than this?"

So I buttered it, placed it on a dish, and said, "HERE, GIVE THIS TO THAT DING-DONG!"

The steward turned around—and guess who was standing directly behind him? You guessed it: the ding-dong himself, Secretary Schlesinger. "Here's your toast, sir," the steward said to him.

I could have died right there.

Vice President Ford

When Vice President Agnew resigned, President Nixon selected Congressman Gerald Ford from Michigan to be his new second-in-command. I was assigned to fly with Mr. Ford on Air Force Two during the following eight months. We traveled to forty of the fifty states to give the American people an opportunity to get to know their new vice president. Most of our trips were one-day out-and-back missions, with one of our longest days being twenty-two hours. On that trip, we were due to arrive back at Andrews Air Force Base at 6:30 a.m. At 4:00 a.m., Vice President Ford said to me, "John, I'm going to take a nap, so wake me up at 6:00 a.m."

By 10:00 a.m. that same morning, Mr. Ford was out playing eighteen holes of golf while the rest of us were home in bed. He was a veritable iron man. Although his stay in office was short lived, he will go down in history as a decent, moral man who brought dignity and stability back to our government during one of its darkest times.

To John Haig, with appreciation and warmest best wishes. Gerald R. Ford

Prime Minister of India

Later on, I was part of a challenging and most unusual trip: transporting the prime minister of India, Morarji Desai, for five days. We were given two weeks to prepare, during which time we met with representatives of the Indian government, the US State Department, and the White House.

After finding out the likes and dislikes of the prime minister and staff, we met with the proprietor of an Indian-American restaurant who had been commissioned to prepare many of the foods (specifically, vegetarian and meat entrees).

During the trip, the restaurateur prepared such items as fresh carrot juice, watermelon juice, Indian sweets, and breads. Special vegetarian platters were made for half of the delegation, and meat platters for the rest. What a combination of foods! Prime Minister Desai was an elderly gentleman with a unique background. He was eighty-two years old, and he had four children. At age thirty-two, he had become celibate and had remained that way. He would consume approximately five cloves of fresh garlic each day with his meals, and he would drink a container of his own urine (ugh!). This was, of course, served to him by his attending physician—not the Air Force Stewards (thankfully).

He would consume approximately five cloves of fresh garlic each day...

Air Force One Backup Trip

On June 10, 1974, I departed Andrews Air Force Base on my first Air Force One backup trip with President Nixon. The president flew aboard the primary Air Force One aircraft, tail number 27000, a 1972 model Boeing 707. I was assigned to the backup aircraft, a 1962 model Boeing 707, tail number 26000, carrying the extra White House staff members, plus State Department personnel. This was the aircraft that had brought back President Kennedy's body from Dallas the day he was assassinated. And Vice President Lyndon Johnson had been sworn in as president on the same aircraft before returning to Washington.

Our menus on the backup aircraft were the same as the primary. This was done so that if there was a problem and the president had time to switch aircrafts, the meals would stay the same. The pilot of the backup aircraft was Air Force Lieutenant Colonel Lester McClelland, from Pennsylvania. I approached him and asked what part of Pennsylvania he was from.

"Masontown," he said.

I excitedly told him that I was from McClellandtown, which was only three miles from Masontown. It turned out that his uncle had been my high-school principal. Lieutenant Colonel McClelland had been a star football player in high school and then an All-American at Syracuse University, later playing in the Canadian Football League. Even then on board the plane, he was a strapping six feet five, and he weighed about 260 pounds. Later on, someone else mentioned that Lieutenant Colonel McClelland didn't fly the airplane, he wore it. He was a good leader and a great pilot.

The flight engineer on the primary aircraft was a gentleman named Chief Master Sergeant Joe Chappell, who happened to be on board the aircraft transporting President Kennedy's body back from Dallas.

Our next stop was Cairo, where we visited and went inside the largest pyramid (Cheops). President Nixon invited President Anwar Sadat to accompany him aboard Marine One, and they landed near the pyramids. After landing, President Nixon presented the helicopter to President Sadat as a gift from our government.

We then flew on to our next stop, Jeddah, the gateway to Saudi Arabia on the shores of the Mediterranean Sea, for a short visit, and then on to Damascus, Syria. The most fascinating part of the trip for me was Tel Aviv, Israel. We traveled to Jerusalem and walked the Via Dolorosa (the Way of the Cross) to Golgotha where Christ was crucified. As a Christian who attends the Catholic Church, this was a realistic reminder of the Stations of the Cross that I participate in during the Lenten season each year. We also visited the Wailing Wall, Dome of the Rock, and then Christ's birthplace in Bethlehem. What a pilgrimage!

The last stop on this whirlwind nine-day trip was Amman, Jordan, before we finally returned to America. I was so impressed with flying the backup aircraft that I set a goal to become a permanent member of the Air

Force One flight crew. I liked the idea of flying the same aircraft with the same passengers on every mission.

On a side note, the "Air Force One" call sign came about in the late 1950s during the Eisenhower administration. An Eastern airliner was taking off out of National Airport (currently Reagan National Airport), and at the same time, President Eisenhower's aircraft was taking off out of Andrews Air Force Base, Maryland. The call signs of the aircraft got mixed up by the air traffic controllers, so from that day forward, they decided to call the presidential aircraft "Air Force One."

My opportunity to serve on this historic airplane did not come for a few more years. But I continued to fly many more memorable trips.

Aircraft Carrier Landing

In April 1975, we traveled to Corpus Christi, Texas, with a group of Russian admirals. These Russian naval men were taken aboard the USS *Lexington* aircraft carrier—referred to as the "Lex" or "Lady Lex" by its crew members, the same as she'd been called during World War II. My fellow crew members and I were invited to fly in a Navy COD and land several times on the deck of the carrier. When they told us to strap in for landing, they weren't joking! The plane landed at full speed, just in case its tailhook missed. If the tailhook had missed, we would have been airborne again in seconds. Whatever negative thoughts I might have had about Navy pilots before that day were put aside. Anyone who could land an aircraft on what, from a distance, appears to be a postage stamp out in the ocean—moving back and forth with the waves—was okay with me.

Sadly we couldn't stay on the carrier because Charlton Heston and a film crew were on board filming the movie *Midway*.

Funeral Trip with Ms. Lillian Carter

President Carter selected his mother, Ms. Lillian Carter, to be his official emissary to the funeral of Pope John Paul I, which was religious history in the making for me. Guests who traveled with her included Governor Ella Grasso (first female governor of Connecticut), Mayor Ed Koch of New York City, Senator Thomas Eagleton (former vice presidential candidate), and a number of others.

During the flight, Ms. Lillian hosted a poker game, playing with Governor Grasso, Mayor Koch, and several others—and she managed to win their money. Later, in her wonderful Southern accent, Ms. Lillian told the steward, "About thirty minutes before I have my suppah, pour me a drink of bourbon, and make it strong enough where I can taste it." And that was exactly what we did!

On the day of our departure back to Washington, I received a call saying that Ms. Lillian and her party would arrive at the aircraft in forty-five minutes, and to please be prepared to serve dinner right away. Moving quickly, I placed the chicken a l'orange in the convection oven so that it would be ready to serve

when they arrived. We were indeed ready to serve in forty-five minutes, but then we received another call saying that Ms. Lillian and her party would be delayed an additional forty-five minutes. Guess what happens to chicken that continues to bake in its own juices even after the oven heat is turned off? The bright orange sauce looked like burnt caramel. We had no other choice but to serve it, and much to our delight, they liked it. But it was still hard to live down because a fellow steward, my buddy, told the whole Western world about the incident when we returned home.

Upon our arrival back home, Ms. Lillian thanked each crew member for a job well done, and then said, "Y'all took very good care of me, and I plan to tell Jimma when I return to the White House."

Vice Presidential Trip to China

One day in August 1979, I had lunch at a restaurant near the base, where many of my fellow crew members would go to eat. As I was leaving and walking to my car, I heard a voice calling to me. When I turned around, I saw that it was the chief steward of Air Force One.

"The job on Air Force One is yours if you still want it," he said.

I was so taken aback that I asked him to repeat himself. He said it again, then told me that the job might only last until the end of President Carter's term in office, and that we all worked at the pleasure of each administration. I told him on the spot that I accepted—but I still had to make one more trip to China with Vice President Mondale.

It was a long flight to China, with stops in Guam, Japan, and finally Beijing, where the temperature was quite comfortable. Making the trip even

more memorable was a special invitation in my room, which stated, "On the occasion of the visit to China by the Honorable Walter F. Mondale, Vice President of the United States, and Mrs. Mondale, Vice Premier Deng Xiaoping requests the pleasure of your company at a banquet of the Great Hall of the People at 7:30 p.m. on Sunday, August 26, 1979."

On that evening, we sat at large circular tables seating ten persons each: five Americans and a Chinese interpreter for each one of us. The following dinner was served:

M E N U

Hors d'Oeuvres

Consomme of SiLver Agaric

Cream of Three Delicacies
(Fish Maw, Pigeon Eggs
and Sea Cucumber)

Steamed Beef

Mushrooms and Cane Shoots

Duck Slices in Brown Sauce

Ice Cream in Three Flavours

Pastries

Fruits

When we returned from the banquet, we found another invitation in our rooms: "On the occasion of the visit to China by the Honorable Walter Frederick Mondale, Vice President of the United States of America, and Mrs. Mondale, the Cultural Ministry of the People's Republic of China invites you to a performance of music, dance, and the Beijing Opera, presented jointly by the Chinese Opera and Ballet Company, and the 4th Troupe of the Chinese Beijing Opera Company at the theater of the Great Hall of the People at 7:30 p.m., August 27, 1979."

A tour had been arranged the following day to see the Great Wall, Summer Palace, Ming Tombs, and Forbidden City. So, the next evening after spending the day souvenir shopping and sightseeing, we enjoyed the opera and ballet performance, and I returned to my room later on—only to find yet another invitation in my room: "The Vice President and Mrs. Mondale request the pleasure of your company, Mr. Haigh, at dinner on Tuesday, August 28, at 7:30 p.m., Great Hall of the People (North Gate)." So off I went the next night to dinner. The following menu was served:

DINNER

Hors d' Oeuvres
Consomme of West Lake Greens
Jinhua Abalone
Prawns in Red Sauce
Almond Jelly
Pastries
Fruit

One thing I learned to do rather proficiently from all this dining experience was how to handle chopsticks with the best of them. I also experienced drinking the Chinese version of our white lightning. When you drank it, you toasted in Chinese saying, *"Gombay."* Then you took a drink and made sure that there wasn't a drip left when you turned the glass upside down. They considered that a good toast.

The next morning, as we were having breakfast in the hotel restaurant, all our heads turned to see the biggest, tallest men I have ever seen in one group. It happened to be the NBA World Champion Washington Bullets, who were on a world tour. What a trip!

CHAPTER 2

IN SERVICE TO PRESIDENT JIMMY CARTER
(SEPT. 1, 1979 – JAN. 20, 1981) ///////////////////////

SEPTEMBER 1, 1979, was my first day of duty as a permanent member of the Air Force One flight crew—and a day I will never forget. A person could only attain such a position after being selected by their peers—and after first having the required security clearance, flying experience, and ability to work and serve well with others.

Mount St. Helens
The eruption of Mount St. Helens volcano in Washington state was one of

With Best Wishes to John Haigh

Jimmy Carter

the major disasters of 1980. After all the devastation had settled, President Carter paid a visit to the disaster area. We flew over top of the volcano, giving us the chance to look down at the affected area. The volcano had really blown its top, to a span of three miles across the opening—an amazing yet horrifying sight to see.

One of my fellow crew members had a cousin who was a *National Geographic* photographer, and he had taken several pictures from a helicopter, so he gave us copies.

The First Lady

During President Carter's last year in office, Ayatollah Khomeini captured fifty-two American hostages and the president made a decision not to do any campaigning until the hostages were released. Meanwhile the first lady took over campaigning for him, speaking on his behalf along with her agenda on mental health. As a result of her efforts, Mrs. Rosalynn Carter was inducted into the National Women's Hall of Fame. The press dubbed her the "Steel Magnolia." And the old saying is that behind every good man is the woman who supports him—and she did that well. Traveling from one end of the country to the other with Mrs. Carter gave us the unique opportunity to know her well. And she was indeed quite a lady!

To John Haigh,
Best Wishes —
Rosalynn Carter

President Carter Campaigns

Shortly before the election, the president decided to do some campaigning, but it was to no avail. Three days before the vote, the only people that showed up at some of the rallies were families of the band members who were playing the music. We felt that President Carter and his staff knew before election night that they were losing, and as a result, he conceded early on that night.

President-Elect Reagan Trip

I was selected to take charge of the trip to pick up President-Elect Ronald Reagan and Mrs. Reagan at Los Angeles International Airport, California. The first thing that got everyone's attention was when reporter Sam Donaldson tried to get closer to the new president-elect to ask questions, and one of Mr. Reagan's senior aides yelled at Sam to get back behind the press barrier or else he'd have his press privileges pulled. Sam wasn't used to that because he had gotten away with it plenty of times during the previous administration.

...I have enough work to keep me busy for the next four years...

President-Elect Reagan was asked if he planned to do a lot of traveling during his term in office, and in his famous relaxed style, he answered, "Well, I have enough work to keep me busy for the next four years in Washington. That's why I have a vice president and all my ambassadors to do my legwork."

White House Christmas

In December 1980, all of the Air Force One flight crew and office personnel were invited to the annual Christmas celebration. It was held outside, and we were entertained by Olympic gold medalist Peggy Fleming. A portable

ice rink had been assembled for her performance, which she did most gracefully. Before departing the grounds,
I saw the first lady standing nearby, so I
took my wife Phyllis over to meet her.
Mrs. Carter was gracious and made
some nice comments about our travels together and how well we'd taken
care of her. Phyllis, of course, was pleased to meet her as well.

A portable ice rink had been assembled...

President Carter's Final Flights

Historically the newly inaugurated president lends Air Force One to transport the former president back to his home. This time, it would be slightly
different. During his last year in office, President Carter had spent a great
deal of time trying to get the hostages released from Iran. He'd received
the ultimate slap in the face when they released the hostages shortly after
President Reagan took the oath of office. The hostages had been held cap-
tive for 444 days.

So, instead of taking President Carter
right home, we flew him and his party to
Germany, where he met with the hostages
for an emotional visit. The whole world was
with them in their thoughts. It was a long
and memorable twenty-seven-hour day for
the flight crew. Afterward, we flew President Carter back to Georgia and
finally we returned to Washington DC. President Carter had gotten off
the aircraft without saying good-bye to anyone. On the return flight to
Washington, Vice President Mondale invited each crew member into the
state room for a photo opportunity. We found out later that the official
photographer didn't have any film in his camera, so we missed out on
the picture.

It was a long and memorable twenty-seven-hour day...

Shortly before our arrival at Andrews Air Force Base, I sat down at my landing position, near the rear door, and wouldn't you know it, I fell asleep. And of course, one of my fellow crew members ran to get one of the White House photographers to take my picture for posterity.

CHAPTER 3

IN SERVICE TO PRESIDENT RONALD REAGAN

(JAN. 20, 1981 – JAN. 20, 1989)

President Reagan Goes to Cancun

In late 1981, President Reagan made his first overseas trip, to Cancun, Mexico, for an international summit. After the president and his party had departed the aircraft, we taxied the 707 to an area where the leaders of develop-

ing nations had parked their aircraft. We noticed that their aircraft were DC-10s and 747s, all of which dwarfed the size of our aircraft. In fact, the other planes were so large that our 707 could have fit inside of one of them

with room to spare. As a result, a high-ranking member of the president's staff made a decision to order new airplanes to be built. So we were tasked with developing a statement of need for two aircraft companies: the Boeing Company and McDonnell Douglas. This would be the beginning of the ten-year acquisition process for the new aircraft.

Funeral for Princess Grace

In 1982, Mrs. Reagan was invited to attend the funeral of Princess Grace of Monaco. She was accompanied by the Honorable Richard Thornburgh, Governor of Pennsylvania, along with fellow representatives from Pennsylvania. The flight crew stayed in a beautiful Victorian hotel on the French Riviera in Nice, France, which offered the nearest airport location to Monte Carlo. We checked into the hotel, then rode up to our room in an old-fashioned elevator with the entry-gate type of door that you could see through. Six of us rode the elevator, and I stood in the rear, next to what I thought was a wall. When the elevator stopped on our assigned floor, the door opened. The only problem was that the door ended up being what I thought was a wall behind me! I fell backward into complete darkness—what a surprise! That was hard to live down.

In the harbor of Nice, we could see everything from fishing boats to the finest yachts—kind of an international port for the rich and famous. The food was great, and the scenery was spectacular. During the return trip to Washington, I had a conversation with Governor Thornburgh, and told him that I was a constituent and that my family resided near Pittsburgh. He took note of my name and asked for my mom's telephone number, saying that he would like to call her when he returned to his office. Several days later, I got an excited call from my mom telling me all about the governor's call, which was a kind gesture to her.

President Reagan's 73rd Birthday Trip

We enjoyed a special day in the life of President Reagan, as it was a special privilege for us to be part of his birthday celebration trip to Rockford and Peoria, both in Illinois. While in Peoria, he motorcaded to nearby Dixon, Illinois, where a luncheon was held at his boyhood home. Later that same day, we flew to Las Vegas and held another birthday party in flight for him, which was a rare moment. I watched him in awe as he stood over the lighted cake, looking like an excited child, then making a wish and blowing out the candles. Afterward he cut and served the first piece, and then reminisced about the day's events. One of the staff members asked what he wished for. He paused for a moment and then said, "Peace in Lebanon."

I took over serving the rest of the cake, and accidentally got the corner of my blazer decorated with icing. The president saw what had happened to me and said, "Don't feel bad; I once fell into a cake." That made me feel a little better.

"Peace in Lebanon"

Then the staff was telling a cute story about Mickey Rooney. A movie director wanted to do the story of Mickey Rooney's life and was having trouble finding someone to play the lead role. Someone said, "Why not use Mickey Rooney himself?" The President spoke up and said, "Oh, no! He's too short."

Mrs. Reagan's Baggage

During the presidential campaign, an important piece of Mrs. Reagan's baggage got lost. The luggage contained the gown that she had planned to wear for the evening's main event. From that day forward, she was fussy about who handled her bags. For example, while taxiing after our arrival at Andrews Air Force Base from a trip to California, Mike Deaver, the deputy chief of staff, walked into her state room and picked up one of her bags to assist her. She told him to leave her bags alone, that she didn't trust him.

"I trust John," she said.

He looked at her and said, "O ye of little faith."

So, with her trust in me, I got to handle her bags often—even if things still didn't always go as smoothly as I would have hoped. One time, Mrs. Reagan asked me to bring her one of her bags, and I said, "You mean the purple one?"

"That's not purple; that's red!" she said.

"Yes, ma'am, that's red!" I said.

Air Force One: The Planes and the Presidents

On June 25, 1983, filmmaker Eliott Sluhan shot an interview with President Reagan aboard Air Force One while flying to Chicago. It was to be part of a documentary that had been planned for twelve years. Originally conceived along with newsman and Cinerama producer Lowell Thomas, Elliott dedicated the film to Thomas for his longstanding enthusiasm for aviation. The film was titled, *Air Force One: The Planes and the Presidents.*

I was excited to be standing behind the cameraman who stood in the doorway to the state room during the filming. I was simply in awe of history in the making, as Elliott Sluhan and former press secretary to President Ford, Mr. Jerald terHorst, conducted the interview with President Reagan. With the documentary film, Elliott did an outstanding job presenting Air Force One to the world, and he became a permanent member of the Air Force One family to those of us who know him. We were even invited

For John Haig
Best wishes

to the National Air and Space Museum for the grand opening of the production. Charlton Heston narrated the documentary, and he was gracious enough to send me a signed photo through Elliott.

Paris G-7 Summit

Each year, the heads of state from the nations with the largest economies meet for an international summit. First it was called the G-6, for "Group of Six," then G-7 and now currently G-8. In 1982, it was still the G-7 Summit, and the leaders met in Versailles, a suburb of Paris, France. Rooms were arranged for the flight crew at the Sheraton Hotel. We were briefed to always travel with two or more people when sightseeing. We enjoyed our time visiting the Eiffel Tower, Arc de Triomphe, Moulin Rouge (music hall), and Place Pigalle (a famous public square), as well as a scenic tour by way of a large excursion boat floating down the Seine, taking us from one end of Paris to the other. Another highlight from the trip was dining at an American-style restaurant that had been opened by an African-American gentleman who'd stayed in Paris after World War II and opened his own eatery.

An interesting thing happened to me while walking one day and carrying the radio we had been issued for our stay in Paris.

"Base to Haigh," the dispatcher said

"Haigh to base," I said into the radio.

The next thing I heard, rather abruptly, was, "Verify, verify!"

I think they must have thought I was Secretary of State Alexander Haig, who was with the president at the time.

Queen Elizabeth

Once, for twelve most unusual days, Her Majesty Queen Elizabeth and His Royal Highness Prince Philip, the Duke of Edinburgh, were guests aboard the president's backup aircraft. During that time, we dubbed ourselves "Her Majesty's Crew." We picked up Her Majesty and party at Lindbergh Field in San Diego, California, and flew them to Palm Springs, California, where they were to visit with Walter Annenberg, former ambassador to Great Britain, at his Sunnyland Estate.

Speaking of life's humorous moments, these folks were the most proper, stiff-upper-lipped, jolly-good-show type of people you'd ever want to meet. For example, I asked Sir Philip, the queen's apparent "ambassador to protocol," if I could take his coat and umbrella, and hang them in the closet. He looked at me and said, "You may take them ooooonly if you promise faaaaithfully to return them." And he said it all while speaking with a finely tuned British accent, with subtle sincerity. You had to be there. It was all I could do to restrain myself from smiling, but I loved to hear him talk.

We had received an in-depth briefing as to the proper protocol when addressing the queen and her party. Upon seeing her or Prince Philip for the first time, we were not to speak to them until spoken to first, and then we could address them as "Your Majesty" or "Your Royal Highness," then "Yes, ma'am," "No, ma'am," "Yes, sir," and "No, sir."

One time, Prince Philip was walking through the aircraft with his hands folded behind him, looking at the pictures on the wall of the president at different events. When he arrived at the rear galley, he made the comment, "I see you chaps stay in good favor with your boss by displaying his photos throughout the aircraft." He paused for a moment and then said, "But you do have to change them every four years, don't you?"

As the prince turned to walk away, his head of security looked at us and said, "That was a wicked shot!"

We later flew the queen and her party to Santa Barbara, where they were motorcaded to the president's ranch and served a Mexican platter for lunch. One of the president's staff members asked the queen how she liked the Mexican food.

"The tackos were good," the queen said.

"Oh, no, Your Majesty, they are pronounced 'tacos.'"

Then she said, "The used beans were also very good."

"Oh, no, Your Majesty, they are called 'refried beans.'"

The next leg of this historic trip was a stay in San Francisco, where the president hosted a state dinner for them, with entertainment provided by Tony Bennett. Before landing there, we experienced an extraordinary act of flying agility, which took place when our aircraft flew at a low level above the top span of the Golden Gate Bridge. There were lots of oohs and aahs! We made three passes over the bridge, and during the third pass, Her Majesty came out of the state room and knelt to take pictures out of the window—photos of her yacht *The Britannia* as the plane approached the Golden Gate. As the queen was kneeling, her ladies in waiting knelt beside her, as though they had been commanded to do so. And while the queen took photos out the window, the duke was taking pictures of her taking pictures. During our last pass over the bridge, photographers waited below at many strategic locations, including in helicopters, to capture Air Force One, the bridge, and *The Britannia* all in the same photo. The *San Francisco Chronicle* displayed the photo on the front page the next day.

On a side note, President and First Lady Reagan celebrated their thirty-first wedding anniversary in a romantic setting aboard *The Britannia*, with the San Francisco skyline as a backdrop.

As far as the menu planning for the aircraft, we knew that we would be competing with many top-ranked chefs working diligently to prepare the finest meals. We did our research to find out what was being served and tried not to duplicate any meals. Dinner was served on the aircraft, which included the following:

DINNER

Stuffed Cornish Game Hen
Wild Rice
Buttered Broccoli
Roll/Butter
Orange Cake

Air Force One

The meal was served on china made by the Pickard China Company in Antioch, Illinois, with each plate trimmed in gold and featuring an embossed great seal of the United States. The silverware was Gorham Chantilly sterling silver. The meal itself was well received by all.

On the last day of the trip, Her Majesty thanked the crew for a job well done and took a picture with each of us.

Chinese Premier Zhao Ziyang

In January 1984, we hosted the Chinese premier aboard the Air Force One backup aircraft, which Queen Elizabeth had so enjoyed flying. The premier did not speak English, so all communication took place through

an interpreter. Each day, his aide would approach me and make a gesture to get my attention. He would then bend over, grasp his foot, and point to the location where the in-flight booties were kept. The premier relaxed by removing his shoes and donning a pair of these booties. That told me that he was making himself at home away from home. He appeared to enjoy all the perks and graciousness of the presidential state room.

Later on, as I pondered our experiences with the premier and Her Majesty the queen, I realized that these had been incredible moments for me. On one hand was the non-elected head of state, and on the other, the head of state of a sleeping giant—a country that is only 6 percent larger than the United States in land, but five times the population.

From Hawaii and Virginia to San Francisco and New York, the Chinese delegation was warmly received. The following is one of the menus served to the premier and his party:

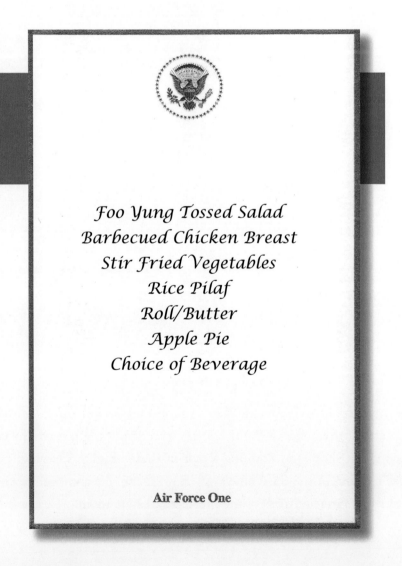

Foo Yung Tossed Salad
Barbecued Chicken Breast
Stir Fried Vegetables
Rice Pilaf
Roll/Butter
Apple Pie
Choice of Beverage

Air Force One

Reelection Kickoff Trip

February 29, 1984, represented not only the historic event of a Leap Day that happens every four years, but also the Iowa kickoff campaign for the Reagan-Bush ticket in that election year. We traveled first to Waterloo, Iowa, where President Reagan addressed the National Cattle Congress, and then on to Des Moines to pay tribute to station WHO, where he had been an announcer many years before.

When they opened the front door of the aircraft in Waterloo, an enthusiastic crowd of at least 15,000 supporters greeted the president. They released thousands of red, white, and blue balloons, and were playing Lee Greenwood's "God Bless the USA," which brought tears to our eyes.

President Reagan's Trip to China

The historic China trip took us first to Seattle, Washington; then the president's ranch for three days; Honolulu, Hawaii, for two days; Guam for one day; and finally to our stop in Beijing, China.

On the flight from Hawaii to Guam, we served a Polynesian style meal of sweet-and-sour chicken, carrots, and celery, all mixed on a bed of rice inside a half pineapple shell. We placed a pair of chopsticks alongside the silverware so everyone could practice eating with them. They would need all the necessary practice possible for the big feeds at the Great Hall of the People in Beijing.

The meal went over very well with one exception: the chopsticks came in a wrapper that said "Made in Taiwan." We had taken the wrappers off the chopsticks in the front end of the aircraft, but they forgot to take them off in the rear before serving the press. The press, sadly, blew everything out of proportion and made it a question of political concern. We found out what they were doing and went straight to the folks that were writing the article,

...the chopsticks came in a wrapper that said "Made in Taiwan"

explaining that this was an honest mistake by the little guys (the peons). We had always done everything with the intent of doing a good job and providing the best service possible to these folks, not knowing if what they were going to say would come back to haunt us. We tried to reason with them, but they still reported it anyway. I guess anything goes when reporting the news. We called it "biting the hand that feeds you." The article appeared in *TIME Magazine* that same week.

The most interesting part of our trip took us to Xian (we called it the Chinese Dust Bowl). It was a two-hour flight, taking us over many mountain ranges. About twenty minutes before arrival, at an altitude of approximately 10,000 feet, it looked as though we were entering a giant dust storm. It was so thick you could feel it inside the aircraft. It gave you the feeling of a loss of air—a shortness-of-breath sensation. As we got closer to landing, we could see dust covering everything in sight. We were told that the dust came from the Gobi Desert.

> *...we could see dust covering everything in sight*

It was a three-hour roundtrip by car for our party to visit the location we were to see. The site was an archaeologist's dream find. They had uncovered 2,000-year-old life-sized terra cotta statues of soldiers of the emperors in all the different battle dresses of their time. Some people made comments that it looked like the statues could come to life at any moment.

On the return trip to Beijing, we served a steak dinner and received rave reviews from the same folks that so vividly described the chopsticks *faux pas* to the world. I guess they were pleased to eat a good old-fashioned piece of beef after eating Chinese delicacies for a few days.

The next stop was Shanghai, a lovely place where the hotel was more American-style, with beautiful surrounding gardens and a climate much like that of Norfolk, Virginia. Menus offered writing in both Chinese and English. The people dressed in more of a variety of colors.

On the morning of departure, the flight crew was congregating outside the hotel, waiting for transportation to the airport. A funny incident happened involving a fellow crew member and me. I had been trying for several days to get someone to sign my name in Chinese on my Great Wall certificate, verifying that I had made the climb. I finally got Mr. Li, our assigned interpreter, to do it. I set my briefcase on the ground, then he and I kneeled down. Looking at me, he asked what my name was and I said, "John Haigh." I thought he was going to sign it in Chinese, but instead, as I said my name, he began writing it in English. I had a look of dismay on my face at that moment, which was immediately recognized by a fellow crew member—and that did it! The other crew member started jumping up and down, laughing and yelling, telling everyone in sight, "Did you see John's face when Mr. Li signed his name?" Just the day before, I had heard a story about an American diplomat from the past who had made a gesture of some sort and embarrassed a high-ranking Chinese official—which led to a twenty-year break in diplomatic relations. With this information in mind, and watching my fellow crew member acting up, I got upset, thinking that we might possibly be causing another international incident. What got me most, though, was that I wanted to laugh along with them, but was afraid to. However, I ended up getting my certificate signed in English and Chinese.

Did you see John's face...?

We departed Shanghai without incident (thank goodness) and headed for Alaska. We started the flight by surprising everybody with the menu of the day, which comprised scrumptious Chinese delights. Having discussed these items in jest the day before, we decided to have a little fun with it, just to see the looks on their faces:

Shark Fin Soup
Foo Yung Tossed Salad
Liver of Peking Duck Pâté
Chicken Chow Mein
Pork Fried Rice
Orchid Fruit Parfait
Choice of Beverage

Air Force One

We heard a lot of "You've got to be kidding! Now what's on the real menu?" Having received the response we wanted, it broke the ice for a nice return flight. Then we served a bowl of chili con carne and a hamburger for lunch, and later, a nicely prepared and well-received surf-and-turf dinner—all as sort of a "welcome back to America" treat.

Upon arrival at Fairbanks, Alaska, it was raining, and soon I was standing outside the front door with two umbrellas in hand, waiting for the president and first lady. As they stepped out the door, I was juggling both umbrellas, trying to figure out the right thing to do. So I held one over Mrs. Reagan's head, and handed the other one to the president. As we started down the steps, a photographer took a picture that later appeared on the front page of the newspaper, while cameramen filmed footage that ran on all the networks. As the president got close to the bottom step of the boarding ramp, he paused for a moment, then as he was taking the next step, he said something like, "One giant step to home"—a most fitting statement.

The purpose of our stop in Alaska was the president's meeting with the pope. Many of the cardinals, bishops, and lower-ranking clergy stayed in the same hotel. This was most interesting for those of us who were Catholic. President Reagan and Pope John Paul II met at the airport amongst a huge crowd of cheering spectators. The pope's aircraft parked directly in front of Air Force One. Each of the men gave their welcoming speeches to the crowd, then met in private before the pope accompanied President Reagan back to the foot of the Air Force One steps for our departure, which made for a great photo opportunity.

40th Anniversary of D-Day

To commemorate the 40th anniversary of D-Day, we flew to Europe, starting the historic trip by landing in Shannon, Ireland, and staying two nights in Limerick. Whoever nicknamed Ireland the "Emerald Isle" couldn't have described it more beautifully. From the air, it looked as though an artist and engineer did their best to cut out and then place together the land in perfect pieces, coloring them in the prettiest shades of green for one's eyes to behold. Still, I could understand why the Irish immigrants left in search of new dreams in the United States, and at the same time could also understand why Saint Patrick's Day celebrations are held each year with such jubilation.

Driving through the countryside, and pondering over the Irish side of my family heritage (being the grandson of Patrick Murphy, no less), made the trip even more enjoyable for me. Our last day in Ireland was spent in Dublin, where the president and first lady visited his roots in the small village of Ballyporeen. He witnessed the signature of his family in the church records and then visited some of his kin. He even drank a pint of stout beer in the Reagan Lounge of the O'Farrell Pub. It was a nice occasion for everyone. I didn't have the opportunity to trace my own heritage, but I did feel the closeness of my roots that originated in Dublin.

Soon we were off to England. The crew and I again served our country in support of the president's visit to the economic summit meeting in London. On another day in England at 6:00 a.m., I was sipping a cup of Earl Grey English tea at a nice lodge outside the city limits of Oxford, England. That day—June 6, 1984—marked the 40th Anniversary of the Allies' D-Day invasion of Normandy in World War II. On that day, the president joined Prime Minister Margaret Thatcher, French President Francois Mitterrand, Her Majesty Queen Elizabeth II, His Royal Highness Prince Philip, and

a host of other dignitaries as they all paid homage to those who gave their lives in the European Theater of World War II. Seated in the audience that day were veterans who had actually scaled the walls of Pointe du Hoc. President Reagan paid his respects and then met with each veteran after giving his speech. That was a moment to remember!

Down-to-Earth President

Air Force One had just landed at Sky Harbor Airport in Phoenix, Arizona, for an overnight visit. I helped the president put on his coat, and he asked if he could borrow the electric razor from the state room lavatory.

"Most certainly, Mr. President," I said and then placed it in his overnight bag.

The next morning, as we were departing, he chose to go into detail about his morning shave: "You know, as I was shaving this morning, I got about halfway through one side of my face, and the razor went rr-rr-rr-rr and then quit. So I plugged it into the recharging unit, went to eat breakfast, and then finished shaving. It had just enough power to finish the job. I'm going to check and see if it might be the hotel power, or the power on the aircraft that isn't working right."

I asked him if he would like to take the razor with him to his ranch when we arrived in California, and he said, "No, I won't need it. I'm well taken care of there."

I thought to myself, *I'll just bet you are.*

He also mentioned to me that when he would get a new pair of jeans as a young man, he liked to put them on, jump into a pool of water, and let them form-fit to his body. Then he said he still did the same thing as president while at his ranch.

> **"I'm well taken care of there."**

I was in awe that he would take the time to have small talk with me, but that's just the type of man he was: a real down-to-earth and kind person.

"Just Say No"

As an anti-drug advocate, Mrs. Reagan was invited to attend a "Just Say No" function in Tampa, Florida. The event was hosted by Operation Straight, an organization completely funded by parents of the children in the program, with no outside help from the city, state, or federal government. The parents of two of the graduates invited me to come along, as they said they would be making a special presentation to the first lady.

At the event, I learned that the program has a 95 percent success rate. Another real attention-getting moment for me came when a thirteen-year-old girl stood up in front of the audience and spoke to her parents for the first time in five years. She said that she had taken every drug known to man, even getting into prostitution. Then she looked at her parents and said, "I love you, Mom. I love you, Dad." When she was done speaking, there wasn't a dry eye in the house, including the first lady and me.

During that event, I gained greater respect for the first lady as a person, and I was proud to be part of her travel agenda. It was even more personal for me because of my thirteen-year-old daughter at home: I couldn't wait to get home and tell her how much she meant to me.

Cobb Salad

I received a special request from the first lady's office saying that Mrs. Reagan would like to have a Cobb salad for lunch on the aircraft. I learned that each time she stayed at the Beverly Wilshire Hotel in Hollywood, they would serve her a Cobb salad for lunch. We had never served a Cobb salad before this request, so I placed a call to the Beverly Wilshire Hotel and asked to speak to the chef. I told him my situation, and he sent me a list of all the ingredients, along with a picture of what the finished salad looked like. Soon enough, we duplicated the recipe, and Mrs. Reagan was very pleased.

Interestingly, tradition has it that the Cobb salad was named after Robert H. Cobb, the owner of the Brown Derby Restaurant on Wilshire Boulevard in Los Angeles. The dish was created in 1937. Following are the ingredients to serve four people:

COBB SALAD

½ head of romaine
½ head of Boston lettuce
1 small bunch of curly endive
½ bunch of watercress (coarse
    stems discarded)
[All lettuces should be rinsed, spun, or
    patted dry, and coarsely chopped]
6 slices of bacon
2 ripe avocados, seed removed,
    peeled, and cut into ½-inch
    pieces
1 whole skinless chicken breast
    (about ¾ pound total), halved,
    cooked, and diced

1 tomato, seeded and chopped fine
2 hard-boiled eggs, separated, the
    yolk finely chopped
2 tablespoons chopped fresh
    chives
1/3 cup red wine vinegar
1 tablespoon Dijon-style mustard
1-2 teaspoons sugar
Salt and pepper
1/3 cup olive oil
½ cup finely grated Roquefort

In a large salad bowl, toss together well the various lettuces and watercress. Cook the bacon in a skillet on medium heat until crisp on both sides. Remove from the skillet and lay out on paper towels to absorb the excess fat. Allow the bacon to cool. Crumble the bacon and set aside.

Compose the salad. Arrange the chicken, bacon, tomato, and avocado decoratively over the greens, and garnish the salad with the grated egg and chives.

In a small bowl, whisk together the vinegar, mustard, salt, and pepper to taste, then add the oil in a slow stream, whisking the dressing until it is emulsified. Stir in the Roquefort. Add sugar to taste, ½ teaspoon at a time. Whisk the dressing. Serve separately, toss in with the salad.

Lady Di's Wedding

On a Friday while in the States, I received a rather excited phone call from the flight steward overseeing the mission of taking the first lady to the wedding of Lady Diana in London. The steward said that Mrs. Reagan was asking for her jumpsuit, and no one could find it. As it was customary to have a jumpsuit made for the new president and first lady to wear aboard the aircraft, I told him that I would check into it and let him know where it was. I called the gentleman in charge of having the jumpsuits made and asked him where the first lady's jumpsuit might be.

"What jumpsuit?" he asked.

After learning that no new jumpsuit had been made for the first lady, I explained to him what was going on and told him to do whatever he had to do to get the jumpsuit made. This was Friday, the day the first lady was leaving for London. She was returning on Monday. So I told the man

that I would tell the flight steward to let the first lady know that her jumpsuit was at the dry cleaners, but that we could get it to her for the return trip on Monday.

The man in charge of the jumpsuits jumped through hoops and had the jumpsuit made then flown to London in time for the return trip. However, the flight steward told me that the trip over to England was tense because every time he went into the state room to take care of Mrs. Reagan, she said, "Everything would be fine if I just had my jumpsuit."

President Reagan's Trip to Quebec

President Reagan had visited Canada on many occasions, but this would be the first time in forty-one years that an American president would visit Quebec City—since President Franklin Roosevelt was in office. At the invitation of Canadian Prime Minister Mulroney, the president was to take part in what was being billed as the Shamrock Summit. While in the city, the president attended a gala at the Grand Theatre de Quebec, participated in private meetings with Mr. Mulroney at the Chateau Frontenac, and signed several joint agreements with the Canadian government in an official ceremony at the Citadelle.

During the presidential visit, I traveled with the first lady on a side trip—which happened to be in Quebec at the same time. The Air Force One crew was on one side of town, and the first lady's crew was on the other side. One night, we had eaten dinner and returned to our hotel room around 7:30 p.m. I was all snuggled down watching TV, and around 8:00 p.m., the phone rang. I picked it up and heard a French-sounding voice on the line. It wound up being the right room but wrong hotel. About fifteen minutes later, the phone rang again: same French voice and right room but wrong hotel. I lay down again, but sure enough, fifteen minutes later, the phone rang and the same scenario played out again. I hung up the phone, thinking that one of my fellow crew members from the Air Force One crew had found out where I was staying and had put up this French person to calling me.

Nothing more happened for several hours, but then all of a sudden, I was awakened by a booming knock on the door. Wouldn't you know it, there waiting was a whole group of Air Force One crew members, wide awake and making a special trip to see me. The first thing they did was trash my room completely, then they drank all the beverages in the portable refrigerator and bar. They stayed long enough to make sure that I was wide awake, and then left me sitting in the middle of my unmade bed.

The first thing they did was trash my room completely...

Pepsi Firecracker 400

In 1984 in Daytona, Florida, the president made history by starting the Pepsi Firecracker 400 NASCAR race. He made the announcement aboard Air Force One, "Gentlemen, start your engines!" Then President Reagan arrived, watched from the audience, and presented Richard Petty with the trophy for winning his 200th NASCAR Winston Cup victory, which was a milestone that will be in the NASCAR history books forever—as well as Air Force One history.

Mrs. Reagan's Atlanta Trip

Mrs. Reagan was invited to attend a luncheon meeting of PRIDE (the Parents Resource Institute for Drug Education), which was holding its tenth annual conference. First ladies from several Latin American countries also attended. We flew her to the event on a Douglas DC-9 aircraft.

After the event was over, the first lady and party were excited to hear that we might get home earlier than expected. Everyone was seated, the aircraft was taxiing, and I was doing my normal safety check throughout the aircraft cabin. I was walking forward to take my seat at the forward cabin door, but as I made my way through the state room, the aircraft suddenly stopped. The right-wing side of the aircraft dipped toward the ground, and at that moment, I leaned toward the first lady's table to make sure that she was okay. She had a concerned look on her face—like "What the heck was that?"—and then her Secret Service detail came to her assistance. The flight engineer had to exit the rear of the aircraft, because the front steps had to be secured so the First Lady could safely deplane.

This incident happened as we were making a right turn on to the taxiway too soon, causing the right landing gear to become mired in the mud. Within fifteen minutes, the air was abuzz with CNN helicopters, and the aircraft was surrounded by airport personnel. Within two hours, an executive jet arrived to take us back to Andrews Air Force Base.

South Dakota Bicentennial Trip

The president attended a bicentennial celebration in South Dakota, during which he rode in a covered wagon, greeted the local folks, and took part in the festivities. On the return trip to Washington, we were granted special permission to do a low-level flyby of Mount Rushmore. Soon the press secretary, Larry Speakes, was giving us the president's reaction to the event, which he termed "the sheer beauty of the America's heartland" after he'd gazed upon it from his aerie at the front of the plane. Then the president came out of his cabin, walked over to a group of staff members, and said, "Are you ready for some poetry?" Whether they were or not, the president proceeded: "'I may gaze on planets born of farther suns, I may greater glories one day see, but today, dear earth, how I love thee." That's what the president thought looking at the country. He said that the poem had been written by a female poet whose name he couldn't recall. The folks listening, including me, remembered his recital as "stirring."

> "Are you ready for some poetry?"

To the Ranch and Back

One day, the president approached Air Force One wearing a sport jacket without a tie, ready to head to his favorite destination: California, his home state. He was pulled toward the plane by First Dog Lucky, who looked anxious to take her first flight. The president came back to an area just forward of the press pool with Lucky in tow.

"I get good reviews or I turn her loose," the president said, pointing at the press and grinning.

They asked if he was leaving Lucky at Rancho del Cielo, and he said that he was, because the ranch had 688 acres and he wouldn't have to keep a leash on her there. "The place is 'dog heaven,'" he said.

"Won't you miss her at the White House?" one of the reporters asked.

"Yes," President Reagan said, "but I'll talk 'em into more trips to California."

Having Lucky aboard made the flight interesting. She was a large frisky animal, with a distinct energy of her own. She was well-behaved, but a little overly friendly at times, especially when one of my coworkers went into the state room to check on the president. As the attendant entered, Lucky was sitting beside the president's table. Then something fell on to the floor. As the attendant bent over to pick up the object, Lucky started licking him up and down his cheek, which drew a hearty laugh from the attendant. The president, being the gentleman he was, tried embarrassingly to intervene and pull Lucky back by the leash. In that little episode, I saw another side of the kindness and personal concern from a man I was so proud to serve.

After our arrival in California, and while we were taxiing to the aircraft parking area at Point Mugu Naval Air Station, my coworker and I were discussing the fact that Lucky had not gone to the bathroom for five hours. We thought it might be a good idea to make a trial run with Lucky out the rear of the aircraft while the president was greeting the welcoming party on the ground. We told the president about our idea, and he said, "Well, if it looks as though she might have to go, I'll turn her over to you."

So he deplaned with Lucky behind him on the leash. It had just stopped raining, and the tarmac was still wet. Everything was fine until Lucky hit the ground. The next thing we saw was Lucky putting her wet paws all over the greeting admiral's white dress uniform. We could see the blood rising in the admiral's neck from embarrassment. The president smoothed things over, then turned and headed toward Marine One. All of the sudden, Lucky stopped. Right there in front of the White House press with the rest of

world watching, Lucky had a nature call. The president stood there patiently with an "I'll be darned" look on his face. He handled it gracefully, boarded Marine One, and headed to the ranch.

On the return trip to Washington, we served one of the president's favorite meals: meat loaf, and macaroni and cheese. Before we served the president, his personal assistant came out of the state room and asked, "The president wants to know if you have any first-class napkins?"

"Which ones, sir?" I asked, not about to tell him that I didn't know what he was talking about.

"You know," he said, "the one with the button hole on one end? He likes to attach it to the top button on his shirt while he is eating."

"Oh, that one!" I said. "I don't have any on board at this time, but I promise to have them available on the next trip."

We served everyone a healthy portion of meat loaf. In fact, it was so large a portion that the press made a comment in their pool report that the meat-loaf looked like a brick. They asked, "If someone dropped a bowling ball and a piece of this meat loaf from the top of the Washington Monument, which one would hit the ground first?" So, on the very next trip, we garnished a dinner plate, placed a real brick on it, and served it to the press secretary, from whom came a loud roar of laughter. "Gotcha!" we said.

Later I explained the first-class napkin situation to a close neighbor, who had a special device on her sewing machine. She agreed to sew button-holes in fifty napkins so that we never had that problem again.

My Moment of Truth

We had a routine trip to California planned—or so I'd thought. I was awakened at around 5:00 a.m. on November 2, 1986, so I turned on the TV and started channel-surfing. I finally stopped when I heard a televangelist preaching a sermon on the Great White Throne Judgment. I knew that the Bible says that you must have ears to hear, and that wisdom begins when you have fear of the Lord. I had been attending the Catholic Church most of my life, and had been listening to God's Word, but until that particular morning, I did not have ears to hear. I was forty-four years old, married, the father of three great kids, working in service to the President of the United States, and totally enjoying my military career. However, I sat up and listened to this very powerful message about the Lord Jesus Christ coming into the world, living amongst mankind, being crucified for our sins, dying, and being resurrected to become the foundation stone (the proof) of why Christianity exists.

Then came the part that hit home with me: Jesus told us that he will return, and that only God the Father knows when. But when Jesus does return, it will be to judge the living and the dead. At that moment, I realized the importance of inviting the Lord Jesus Christ into my life—that it must be personal for all of us. We must do this while we are alive in this world. When we do, Jesus becomes the Savior of our life. If we do not invite him into our life in this world, though, then when he returns to judge the living and the dead, it's too late.

When the reality of this message hit me between the eyes like a sledge-hammer, it brought me to my knees. I repented of my sins and personally invited Christ into my life as Lord and Savior. That was the greatest decision I've ever made. I felt like I was walking two feet off the ground for the next six months, asking myself, "Why doesn't everyone know about this?"

Also, everyone who accepts Christ should find a Bible-based church to attend. I happen to be a Christian who attends a Catholic church. Life has taken on a whole new meaning since that day. As a result, I wrote a gospel song as a testimony. It goes as follows:

"SHINE THROUGH ME"

Shine through me, dear Jesus, shine through me
Show me the way, won't you please?
You are the way, the truth, the life, that's for sure
You have opened up my heart forever more

Chorus
Shine through me, dear Jesus, shine through me
You have opened up my heart and set me free
Please be with me every moment every minute of each day
And I will always know you are the way
Shine through me, dear Jesus, shine through me
So others who don't know can learn to see

You'll be with them every moment as you are now with me
Till our spirits join together for eternity

Instrumental
Repeat last two stanzas
Repeat last line and fade

Economic Summit in Venice

The historic trip to Venice, Italy, for the 1987 Economic Summit covered a total of 10,000 air miles. We served prime rib for dinner, and it was well-received. Upon arrival, the official party boarded speedboats docked near the airport, and they were taken into Venice to partake in all the official events.

The flight crew stayed in a nearby town that reminded me somewhat of the village where I lived: with quaint little houses, each having its own driveway entrance, fenced-in yard, and totally surrounded by flowers of all designs. The roses stood out the most. Each dwelling had its own garden that would have made the old Green Grocer—the late Joe Carcione—smile, or I should say, "green with envy." Each of our nine days in Italy were spent in the beauty of this little village, and we tried to learn Italian at the same time.

A visit to Saint Mark's Square—Piazza San Marco in Italian—was one of the highlights of a foray into Venice, which included a tour of the cathedral. We saw thousands of people taking pictures, souvenir shopping, and feeding the pigeons. We also noticed that many people on the streets were being interviewed by the *Good Morning America* film crew.

Before returning to Washington, the president made a short side trip to Rome for a papal visit. Then it was on to Berlin, where President Reagan gave a speech that included the famous phrase "Mr. Gorbachev, tear down this wall!" These words echoed around the world and proved true in the coming years. From Berlin to Bonn, our guests

"Mr. Gorbachev, tear down this wall!"

included Chancellor Helmut Kohl and his family, who were warm and gracious. It was a short visit to West Germany, though, and then it was on to Washington.

I was inspired after President Reagan said those famous words "Mr Gorbachev tear down this wall". I penned the following as a tribute to those words, and it goes like this:

THE WALL IS GONE

Jubilation has arrived, in the place where anger thrived
and peace was a figment of the mind
thousands crossed the barren space, with sighs of freedom on their face
knowing that the wall is gone

Brick by brick they pick and pick, to make their mark be known
of terror that they left behind, the world their light be shown
for others who will follow, with freedoms hope to share
crowning flames of glory, their story left to bear

Years of history yet to come, reflecting times gone by
to those who travel freely, knowing when and why
the world has to grow in love, with freedom as its' pawn
to break the bonds of terror, and know the wall is gone

My Promotion to Chief Steward

A few days after returning from the summit in Venice, my life changed dramatically. I was on leave, making plans with my family, relaxing—no worries. Then I was suddenly called in during leave and told to report to the presidential pilot's office. There, the colonel informed me that I would be taking over as the new chief steward of Air Force One. After catching my breath and settling down, I told the colonel that I would do him a good job, and he said, "I know that." It was an awesome feeling—and an incredible privilege. I was following in the footsteps of my mentor and good friend, Chief Master Sergeant Charlie Palmer, to whom I will be eternally grateful for hiring me. Charlie had been the chief steward for Presidents Nixon, Ford, Carter, and Reagan, for a total of twelve years, and he'd done a fantastic job.

My Expectations as Chief Steward

I had been the deputy chief steward for quite some time under the tutelage of Charlie Palmer, so I was cautiously optimistic about my new position, but very much looking forward with great anticipation to serving the president. One of the first things I did as chief steward was draft a letter of congratulations that would be given to each new steward on Air Force One:

> CONGRATULATIONS again on your selection as a permanent member of the Air Force One flight crew.
>
> Remember … that you were selected by a majority of your peers, along with my blessing, and the final approval of the presidential pilot.
>
> Remember … that we all serve at the pleasure of the current administration.
>
> Never lose sight of the fact that we are the mere transporters of the president and staff from point A to B.
>
> We are not staff members, personal friends, etc., etc., so please use the utmost tact and diplomacy when addressing any passenger.
>
> Each person that occupies a seat aboard the president's aircraft is a VIP, carefully selected by the president's staff. Handle each person the same as you would take care of the president.
>
> When providing service to a passenger or crew member, please put aside any personal problems, irritations, and

aggravations, and give service with a smile. SERVICE … SERVICE … SERVICE … IS OUR BUSINESS. We are the people the passengers come in contact with each flight. The way we treat them is the last thing they are going to remember, regardless of how well the pilot flies the aircraft, or how well the engineers do their thing, or how well the communicators place their calls. We are with them one on one; don't forget its importance.

I do not like to see a passenger have to use a call button to get service.

If you are working the aisle, and make a request for service to a passenger, I expect full galley service, not an argument, such as … who is it for … blah, blah, blah … or any sarcasm. I ABSOLUTELY WILL NOT TOLERATE , UNDER ANY CIRCUMSTANCE, A BAD ATTITUDE.

There are certain crew functions that I expect full participation from our section, especially when a fellow crew member retires.

When everyone is at work, I expect full participation in fulfilling assigned duties, aircraft cleaning, stocking supplies, cleaning the kitchen, cleaning the vehicles, etc., etc. When you are done in your particular work area, help the next person, and the next person, until all the work is finished. Remember, we're all here until the work is done. We're in this thing together. WE ARE FAMILY, WE ARE FLEXIBLE, WE ARE GOOD.

Most importantly, I'm here for you, and I'm very proud to serve with you.

John L. Haigh, CMSgt, USAF
Chief Steward, Presidential Aircrew

The Boeing 707 Air Force One Flight Steward Section consisted of ten permanent members. Whenever a person retired and a replacement was needed, we had a cadre of personnel to draw from, all cleared to fly in support of the president. Whenever the primary and backup aircraft flew an extended trip with the president, we would call upon folks from the support personnel to fly with us. Whenever it came time to replace someone, we would have a crew meeting in which each person would submit a name to be considered, based on a candidate's proficiency to do the job and his or her ability to work and play well with other crew members. On occasion, word would filter back from the pilot's office, wondering how my democratic process was coming along.

There was a time when the flight steward career field was male dominated, especially the Air Force One flight crew. I was part of the crew when the first female flight attendant was selected: Becky Schulz, who did a superb job. She broke that glass ceiling and paved the way for other ladies to follow suit. I was privileged to select the second female flight attendant: Patricia Mysior, who also performed admirably. In addition to Patricia, a variety of people were selected during my tenure as chief steward, such as a Puerto Rican American, Indian (from Bombay) American, and African American. I believed in being fair and provided the same opportunity for all.

Every organization in the Air Force lives by a code and standard of conduct in the performance of their duties. As a flight attendant assigned to the Air Force One flight crew, everyone had an attitude of giving 150 percent of themselves to the customer according to the following information:

Every organization in the Air Force lives by a code...

THE AIR FORCE ONE
PASSENGER BILL OF RIGHTS

★ An Air Force One passenger has the right to courteous treatment from the Air Force One representative at all times and under all conditions.

★ An Air Force One customer has the right to the Air Force One representative's full time and attention each and every flight.

★ An Air Force One passenger has the right to fast and accurate information about our aircraft and service. An Air Force One passenger has the right to have his or her expectations met with full food and beverage service satisfaction.

★ An Air Force One passenger has the right to complain when the service does not meet those expectations and to a prompt remedy when the service is indeed at fault.

★ An Air Force One passenger has the right to expect knowledgeability, resourcefulness, problem-solving ability, concern, and results from those assigned to meet his or her needs.

★ An Air Force One passenger has the right to expect responsiveness and follow- through in emergencies and special situations.

★ An Air Force One passenger has the right to benefits of teamwork in the company he or she deals with, without buck-passing, finger-pointing, or run-arounds.

★ An Air Force One passenger has the right to care, accuracy, and attention to detail in meeting his or her need for Air Force One services.

★ An Air Force One passenger has the right to appreciation on the part of those with whom he or she does business, appreciation both for the service already given and for the service to be given in the future, so long as the passenger bill of rights continues to be observed.

★ Before every flight, everyone knows that their attitude has to be in check: to do their "check up from the neck up" before the president and party arrived at the aircraft. The passengers do not need to know that your car broke down on the way to work, or that you had an argument with your wife/husband or significant other. The only thing Air Force One passengers need to see is your smiling face and great attitude.

Moscow Trip

The president traveled to the USSR, with an en-route stop in Helsinki, Finland, where a Russian military officer joined us for the flight into Moscow, landing at Vnukovo Airport. The president stayed at Spaso House, the ambassador's residence. The flight crew, meanwhile, stayed at the Hotel Rossia, considered to be the largest hotel in the world, with 5,000 rooms.

After we checked in, we went as a group to dinner, where we were entertained by a full orchestra playing "Strangers in the Night" by Frank Sinatra and many other popular songs. To our delight, our hotel was located a short walking distance from Red Square and Saint Basil's Cathedral. We appreciated that Moscow had been home to people like Peter the Great, Stalin, Ivan the Terrible, Lenin, and Trotsky, and at our time of being there, Mikhail and Raisa Gorbachev.

So we arose early the next morning to enjoy breakfast on the 21st floor, with a panoramic view of the city, seeing sites such as the Kremlin, Saint Basil's, the Moskva River with its many bridges, and several of the "Seven Sisters" skyscrapers built during the reign of Stalin. We dined on a variety of foods, including omelets, caviar, and sturgeon, along with a sampling of wine from the nearby Russian state of Georgia. After breakfast, we walked to Red Square to see Lenin's tomb, then observed the changing of the guard and the place where the premier would always stand during the May Day Parade in the square. Directly across from Red Square was a three-story department store called GUM, which housed many shops with a variety of goods from all over Russia. On the street side of the store were many displays of goods in the windows, and I was pleasantly surprised to see a familiar brand of baby formula: Similac with iron.

We toured other areas of the city and saw many memorable sites, such as the Olympic Stadium, the ski lifts, and the soccer stadium. That evening would be remembered by all culture lovers, as we had been invited to the heralded Bolshoi Ballet to enjoy their rendition of *Cyrano de Bergerac*.

...we had been invited to the heralded Bolshoi Ballet...

This theater had produced such greats as Mikhail Baryshnikov and Alexander Godunov. Built in 1856, before the revolution, the theater featured six levels of balconies. We were escorted to our seats by an assigned interpreter. We noticed the extravagant design of the interior, including the ornate crystal chandelier, with small chandeliers around it, that hung from the center of the ceiling above us. Seated only four rows behind the maestro and orchestra, we could feel the years of history around us while sitting in elegant arm chairs, each having an assigned number. Looking around, we could also see that the event was attended by a "who's who" list of Moscow society, including the diplomatic circle.

After the memorable trip to Moscow, we served the following on the president's return flight to Washington, a *piece de resistance*:

Cream Cheese and Pear Salad
Filet of Dover Sole
Lemon and Dill Sauce
Honey Glazed Carrots
Rice Pilaf
Roll/Butter
Key Lime Pie
Choice of Beverage

Air Force One

Reykjavik Summit

The Reykjavik Summit was to be a most historic trip, during which the president would meet with Soviet General Secretary Gorbachev in Iceland at a waterfront home overlooking the Atlantic.

After several days of meetings, the president walked out at the last minute, realizing that Gorbachev was trying to kill the Strategic Defense Initiative, and that ended the summit.

When the passengers came aboard for the return trip to Washington, I said good afternoon to the Chief of Staff Donald Regan.

"What the h--- is good about it?" he replied.

Then the chief of staff told the national security advisor, Admiral Poindexter, to take his place by talking to the White House press in the rear of the aircraft. Chief of Staff Regan said that he was going to have a drink instead. So the admiral was grilled intensely for the next hour and a half.

> ## "What the h--- is good about it?"

Press Secretary's Challenge

The president's press secretary, Marlin Fitzwater, came to me and said he was going to put the Air Force One flight attendants on the spot. I told him that he could have any meal that he wanted, with exception of anything that had to be deep-fried on board. He thought for a moment and then said, "Beef Wellington." I said, "You got it!" We did our homework and got prepared for the next flight, which would take us to Dallas, Texas.

On the return trip from Dallas to Washington, Marlin went back to the White House press and in his best he-man voice said, "You'll be glad to know that the dinner tonight aboard Air Force One was designed by me. I've had it with those wimpy tuna salads on the half-shell."

Here's the menu that Marlin called "the perfect in-flight dinner":

> ## "..the dinner tonight aboard Air Force One was designed by me."

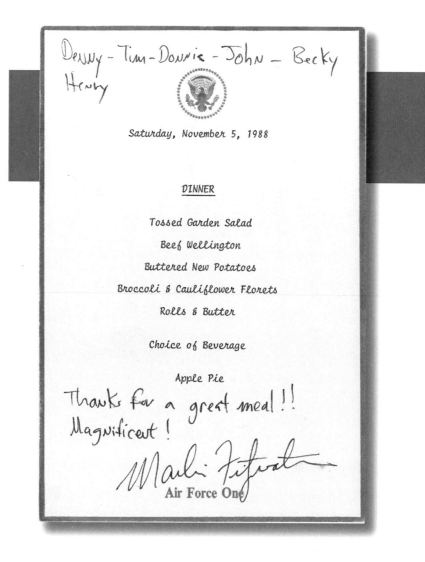

Denny - Tim - Donnie - John - Becky
Henry

Saturday, November 5, 1988

DINNER

Tossed Garden Salad

Beef Wellington

Buttered New Potatoes

Broccoli & Cauliflower Florets

Rolls & Butter

Choice of Beverage

Apple Pie

Thanks for a great meal!!
Magnificent!

Marlin Fitzwater

Air Force One

After everyone had finished their meal, we were given a standing ovation, and Marlin signed a copy of the menu, saying, "Thanks for a great meal. Magnificent."

Sam Donaldson

The White House press traveled on every trip with the president, and the major media outlets would rotate the news anchors on each flight. Sam

Donaldson was a regular traveler on most flights. When we served dinner, we would ask the folks sitting with Sam if we could serve Sam first. Instead of giving Sam a glass of wine, we would give him his own bottle during dinner. He knew we were messing with him, but he liked it.

One of my colleagues once was telling Sam about Willard Scott, the famous weatherman from *Today*, and how Willard was making two million dollars a year. Sam was only making a million and a half on his show with Diane Sawyer.

"You got me," Sam said.

President-Elect's First Trips

President Reagan campaigned vigorously across the country for Vice President Bush in his bid against Governor Michael Dukakis—and the outcome was successful. The Air Force One crew was invited to be in the audience for a hangar arrival at Andrews for President-Elect Bush. It was an awesome experience to be part of all the excitement, waving a flag along with thousands of others.

I was privileged to be on the Bushes' first trip to West Palm Beach, Florida, for a much needed mini-vacation. For their first meal aboard Air Force One, we served them a surf-and-turf dinner that they truly enjoyed. "It's great to travel with the first team," they said to us.

It was an uneventful flight until the arrival at West Palm Beach. As we were taxiing in, the president-elect went into the lavatory to freshen up before greeting the guests in the receiving line. We taxied to a stop, and I took their baggage down to the limousine. When I came back aboard, I noticed that President-Elect Bush had a disgruntled look on his face. I found out after he deplaned that he had been stuck in the lavatory. The door would not open. Thankfully he had managed to make it out through the closet, as it had an exit into the front crew compartment—but he wasn't happy about it.

Several days later, we were returning to Washington. After reaching altitude, I heard the call button for the state room. I went in to find out what they needed, and saw Mrs. Bush sitting alone. I asked if she needed anything, and she said, "No, but George might." Then I heard a noise coming from the lavatory. The door was stuck again! By the time I got to the door and tried to open it, the president had gone through the closet again, then had come out through the crew compartment and back into the State Room.

"Do you think you can get that door fixed?" he asked.

"Yes, sir, Mr. President, I'll take care of it," I said.

On the very next trip, we were on the same aircraft, flying out of Andrews Air Force Base. Shortly after takeoff, the call button went off in the state room. I went to see what they might need, and the first thing I saw was President-Elect Bush with a disgruntled look on his face again. He and the first lady were seated at a table facing each other. I quickly learned that the president's seat, which was supposed to be locked into the floor, had slid backward about four feet

"Yes, sir, Mr. President, I'll take care of it."

into the bulkhead behind him as the aircraft made its initial climb. He looked at me and said, "John, do you think you can get this seat fixed?"

"Yes, sir, Mr. President, I'll take care of it."

Upon arrival at Andrews Air Force Base, I got in touch with the Air Force One chief of maintenance and told him to check everything on that airplane that moved, just in case the president needed to use it. I certainly didn't need strike three!

Oval Office Visit

After traveling all over the world with President and First Lady Reagan for eight years, the flight crew and office personnel were invited to the Oval Office for an official photo. We gathered around the president behind his desk as he reminisced about flying with us. He also shared a number of his famous stories he liked to tell on board the aircraft. I noticed two plaques on his desk. One said, "It can be done." The other said, "There's no limit to what a man can do, or where he can go, if he doesn't mind who gets the credit." Those quotations were good examples of his leadership style. Each year for many years, on Mrs Reagan's birthday, the President would send a dozen red roses to her parents, thanking them for bringing the love of his life into the world. He also said that there is no greater feeling than to be walking up to your house knowing there is someone on the inside waiting to hear your footsteps.

He then took individual photographs with each of us and offered appropriate kudos for a job well done.

Being with President Reagan aboard Air Force One was special, but joining him in the Oval Office was a once-in-a-lifetime experience as well.

To CMSgt John E. Haigh
With best wishes, Ronald Reagan

Air Force One Complex

On January 12, 1989, President and Mrs. Reagan were hosted by Secretary of Defense Frank Carlucci, and Chairman of the Joint Chiefs of Staff, Admiral William J. Crowe, at the grand opening of the new Air Force One Complex at Andrews Air Force Base, Maryland. This was an armed forces review and awards ceremony in their honor, and it included a pre-ceremony concert, arrival fanfare, honors, troop review, inspection, National Anthem, awards, remarks by the hosts, presentation of the US Constitution, a centennial flag, a video presentation of President Reagan's life in office, a response

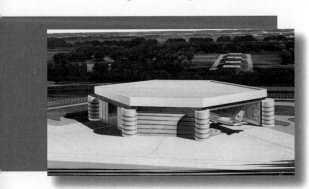

by the president, a pass in review, a flyover, a final musical salute, and a reception. This new state-of-the-art facility would be the home of the new 747s that would take the presidency into the 21st century. What a privilege to be part of the old and new Air Force One aircraft and complexes.

Home to California

On January 20, 1989, President George Herbert Walker Bush was sworn in, and then gave his inaugural address. He then walked former President and Mrs. Reagan to Marine One for their final flight to Andrews Air Force Base. Meanwhile we were watching everything unfold via CNN on the aircraft, awaiting their arrival. The honor guard, cabinet members, White House staff, and many other dignitaries were there for the final sendoff. President Reagan was given a twenty-one-gun salute, then took a final walk in front of the troops and offered a few parting words from a podium before finally boarding the aircraft. As President and Mrs. Reagan reached the top of the steps, they turned around and waved for one last time.

With each change of presidential administrations, the new president loans the former president his aircraft for the final trip home. So, instead of our call sign being Air Force One, it was SAM (Special Air Missions) 27000.

We lifted off at approximately 1:08 p.m. The plane did not fly over the White House, but passed west of the Capitol. The Reagans began working their way through the plane within a few minutes of departure. Reporters conducted an interview with them as they stood in the doorway to the rear press area. Before the interview began, Mrs. Reagan was overheard saying that she had been chilled to the bone, and that it was good to be warm again. The president changed from his suit coat into a blue Air Force One jacket that had his name embroidered on the upper left side.

Shortly before the Reagans appeared, the first lady's chief of staff had presented them a black-and-white picture of the president playing the role of an alcoholic on a GE Theater presentation in the mid 1950s. The caption read, "OK, boss, we're ready for a drink. How about you?" The chief of staff had found the picture while looking through memorabilia at the White House. Later Mrs. Reagan said that the picture showed her husband playing the role of a real person who had been a businessman before becoming an alcoholic, losing his business, and attempting suicide.

Someone aboard commented that President Bush had said that the hardest thing he had to do was fight back the tears as he watched President Reagan leave. In response, Mr. Reagan said, "Well, it's been a time of tears for a great many people, and certainly for us. I appreciate that he felt that way."

The president and first lady spent a long time with the press reflecting on the past eight years, and they shared their thoughts about the future. Mrs. Reagan commented to the press that she wanted to settle the question about the president's taking naps. "Never," she said. "No, in eight years, he never took a nap." On Air Force One, he once had me bring the White House photographer up to the state room when Mrs. Reagan was not on board, just to take a picture of him lying on the couch/bed so that he would have a picture to show her.

During this discussion of taking naps, Mr. Reagan said, "That's a difficult thing. In fact, anyone on the campaign plane will tell you, when I would go back after several stops, and everybody on the plane would be asleep, I'd be the only one awake and walking around. She sometimes gets edgy because she thinks I should be able to take a nap."

"Well, why haven't you ever taken a nap?" one of the reporters asked.

"I just don't do it," Mr. Reagan said.

After the press Q&A session ended, the Reagans went back to the staff area to chat briefly with their small entourage, saying their good-byes to them. Then the following dinner was served before arrival:

DINNER

Tossed Green Salad
Pork Tenderloin w/ Peppercorn Sauce
Green Beans Amandine
Glazed Belgian Carrots
Roll/Butter
Boston Cream Pie
Choice of Beverage

Air Force One

On many occasions when Mrs. Reagan had not been on board, the president would ask what we had for dessert, and I would say, "Mr. President, we're having ice cream." He would say, "I like how you think." He really liked ice cream.

I had written a poem that was inspired by President Reagan, then had it inscribed on a brass plaque and bonded to an Air Force One dinner plate, and then bonded to a circular oak plaque. I had received permission from the president's personal aide and the presidential pilot to present it to Mr. Reagan before arrival in California. A friend of mine, Technical Sergeant George Revoir, did the script writing on the brass plaque, had the oak plaque made for it, did the bonding preparation, and gave it back to me in time for this presentation.

The president's aide wanted the White House press to come forward for the presentation, but I said no, that I wanted it to be private. So the aide took me in to make the presentation. I explained how he had inspired me to write it, and then I said, "Now I give it to you."

The White House photographer took a great picture of me standing between the president and first lady, holding the plaque. They were touched by this gesture, and thanked me graciously. The poem is titled "A Shadow," and it goes like this:

"A SHADOW"

He's a tall man in stature
with an award-winning smile
a commanding voice that reaches out
and touches one and all
He has a way with friend or foe
I know he's surely blessed
I'm just a shadow in his spotlight of greatness

He's traveled all around the world
with his lady at his side
on Air Force One the plane
that flies them safely through the skies
everywhere they go they bring love and tenderness
and I'm proud to be in the shadow of their spotlight of greatness

When we arrived in California, it looked like the beginning of a campaign all over again. We arrived in Los Angeles, the same place I had picked them up for their first trip to Washington eight years earlier. Mr. Reagan's old friend and fellow actor Robert Stack and a host of other dignitaries were there to welcome them home. Mr. Reagan gave a short speech and then motorcaded to their new home in Bel Air.

After the crowd dispersed, we planned to give a show-and-tell of the airplane to comedian Rich Little. As he was coming up the steps, I looked at the copilot, Lieutenant Colonel Danny Barr, and said, "Watch this." Lieutenant Colonel Barr shook hands with Rich Little first, then I shook his hand, saying, "Uh-uh-uh, I-I-I'm J-J-J-Jimmy Stewart." Mr. Little looked at me like I was crazy, but I had to do it one time.

On the return flight to Washington, I thought about the trip we'd just made to California. When I had walked into the state room to secure everything for landing, Mrs. Reagan was sitting in the president's lap, and they were looking out the window, pointing at landmarks in Los Angeles they recognized. I secured everything and walked out, leaving them looking like two high-school sweethearts going to their prom. I also recalled that in the first lady's compartment had been a picture of the two of them at the ranch, lying in a hammock, embracing. I thought to myself that these folks had their home life in order, and the country had been in good hands for the past eight years.

This flight was the end of another chapter in Colonel Bob Ruddick's life as presidential pilot. I had been privileged to work for him for eight years, first as a newly assigned crew member, then as deputy chief steward, and finally as chief steward for the past year and a half. I have always had great respect for him as a leader and a person. The following is a tribute that I was inspired to write about him:

"THE SKIPPER"

The Skipper took the helm of the world's finest plane
making all maneuvers in the Air Force One safety lane
he was tall in the saddle of a great winged steed
much like the president
he always took the lead

He's wound down his tenure of a long reigning career
capping off the ending of the job he held so dear
his leadership was steady
his compassion was grand
most of all the Skipper was a mighty fine man

Having had the privilege and good fortune to work for Ronald Reagan for eight years could only be made better by carrying on in the same capacity as chief steward for President George H. W. Bush. Each president has been known by some type of personal label, such as Ronald Reagan "The Great Communicator." President Bush would go on to be labeled "The Hands-on President."

To CMSgt John Haigh
With best wishes, Ronald Reagan
Nancy Reagan

CHAPTER 4

IN SERVICE TO PRESIDENT GEORGE H. W. BUSH

(JAN. 20, 1989 – JUNE 30, 1992)

Hands-On Man

President Bush motorcaded to Andrews Air Force Base due to heavy fog. Senator Strom Thurmond and Governor Campbell of South Carolina were already seated in the guest compartment of Air Force One. The president walked on board, and his first words were, "First class," in response to the new Air Force One flight jacket draped over his seat, with his name embroidered above the seal of the president. He tried it on, gave his vote of approval, and proceeded toward the rear to greet the guests.

To John Haigh, with best wishes *G. Bush*

He had a breakfast of yogurt with Grape Nuts, and Kava coffee with Hermesetas and skim milk. The rest of the party had fruit and a bagel with cream cheese. We landed and were taxiing toward the passenger terminal when all of a sudden I heard something fall in the state room lavatory. I was standing by outside the lavatory with the president's coat, waiting for him to come out. When he did come out, he said, "John, I'm going to make you a list of needs for the lavatory on the way home."

On the return trip to Washington, I headed toward the state room, where Chief of Staff Sununu was talking to Mr. Bush, to be followed by Governor Campbell. I told my assistant up front to let me know when the governor came out of the state room, as I needed to talk to the president. He looked at me and said, "Do you know what you just said? Do you know how many people in the world cannot do that, and you get to walk right in and talk to him, just like that?"

I agreed: "That's awesome!"

Barbara Bush   Gg Bush

I finally went in to ask the president about the list for the lavatory, and he said, "Let's take a look for ourselves." He went through each drawer, keeping some things and getting rid of others. That was special for him to take time to do that, and it sure made my job a lot easier, taking away the guess work. It also confirmed the fact that he was indeed a hands-on president.

Trip to Bismarck, North Dakota

The president was invited to Bismarck to take part in the dedication of North Dakota's Centennial Grove. The president spoke at Capitol Square and said, "I had no idea when I accepted your invitation to come to Bismarck, that you were going to put me to work planting a sapling. No one told me the sapling in question is twelve-feet tall. This particular elm tree is a descendant of a tree planted on thc White House lawn by John Quincy Adams. Now it and its seedlings will be part of North Dakota forever."

He talked about a man who'd lost his wife and mother in a single day, then came to North Dakota, almost crazy with grief. The man had worked the range in the worst kind of weather, always leading, never following. He'd even worn a sheriff's badge. In short, Mr. Bush told the crowd, Teddy Roosevelt had become a man and a guardian of nature in North Dakota. When Mr. Roosevelt went back East, and back to politics, he took with him an understanding that the seemingly endless resources of the West were being threatened by the exploitation of man. Teddy Roosevelt wrote these words to school children on Arbor Day 1907: "A people without children would face a hopeless future; a country without trees is almost as hopeless."

President Bush then said, "Let us honor the coming birthday of North Dakota, and the memory of the country's first environmentalist by dedicating this centennial fur oak [which was 100 feet from the podium at the three o'clock position) along with this White House elm. Before the year 2000, North Dakota will plant 100 million trees—almost half as many trees in one state as there are Americans in the Union. May each tree add to the abundance of the good life in North Dakota, and cleaner air for North America."

"...North Dakota will plant 100 million trees..."

President's Birthday

It was June 12, 1989, and we were headed for Yellowstone Park on President Bush's birthday. En route, we hosted an Air Force One party, with a beautiful chocolate cake decorated with marzipan, and Korbel champagne for a beverage. We started descending into Yellowstone as the party began, and

the president wielded the cake slicer and then started cutting while we passed out slices to the staff and guests. The press were invited to come forward without cameras—and everyone laughed at that joke. That was like asking them to attend a press conference without being allowed to ask any questions. Everyone enjoyed the festivities, and a few of them enjoyed it so much that they had it all over them.

Once on the ground, the president and his grandson went fishing at Grand Teton Dam.

The flight crew toured the Old Faithful geyser and the areas where the trees had been burned from a recent fire. I walked within twenty feet of a buffalo, and while I was standing there, someone handed me a poster with a buffalo warning that said, "Steer clear because of the potential physical danger. They can run at speeds up to forty miles per hour." That, my friends, got my attention.

Europe Trip

Upon landing in eastern Europe, the president was greeted by a huge crowd at Gdansk, Poland. Then, as the president and first lady rode in a limousine with President Lech Walesa, it was difficult for them to see anything because of the crowds. There were estimated to be as high as a quarter million people lining the streets. Tens of thousands of people waved flags, leaning out of windows, giving "V" signs.

...a quarter million people lining the streets

Mrs. Bush said, "Lech Walesa kept saying to us, 'Oh my gosh, oh, fantastic, fantastic.'"

Back aboard Air Force One, the president summoned one of the Associated Press photographers, Charlie Tasnadi, age sixty-four, who had come from Hungary in 1951. Charlie and his girlfriend, who later became his wife, had crawled under barbwire and through a mine field to escape Hungary. Marveling that he was now returning to Hungary on Air Force One, the president told him that he was happy that Charlie was there, and that it was most fitting and proper that he return this way. Mr. Bush asked if Charlie had any relatives and said that he would be glad to meet any of them. Charlie told him that he had no relatives there, but that his wife did. Charlie was very happy, and he later said, "God bless him for this opportunity to return to my homeland this way."

Later, in Paris, they were celebrating the bicentennial of the French Revolution, which brought forth the rights of man in France. The flight crew stayed at the Sheraton Hotel. As we were entering the hotel lobby, we saw a huge mural on the wall depicting Napoleon and his troops on the battlefield. Our colonel said, "See that fella on the horse? That's me leading the troops."

My deputy looked at the colonel and said, "Do you see the smoke coming up behind that row of trees in the background? That's John and me cooking your dinner—if you make it back."

We all laughed, and the colonel said, "You got me."

Our subsequent trip to the Netherlands marked the first time an American president made an official visit to that nation. President and Mrs. Bush visited the International Church of Leiden, the spiritual home of the pilgrim fathers and of our American ideals. The president told the people in Leiden that history's great wheel was turning once again, just as the winds of hope carried the pilgrims to a new world—a world where the yearning for freedom and democracy flourished for others as it had in this great land, the United States of America.

The Coffee Incident

We were flying an out-and-back trip to New York, and the president was having a meeting with his staff. He asked me for a cup of Kava instant coffee. I served it to him and went back to the forward galley. A few moments later, the call button came on in the conference room, so I went back. The president, with a cocktail napkin in his left hand, was probing at a black speck on the napkin with his right index finger.

"John, what's this look like to you?" he asked me.

By this time, I was swallowing a big "Oh dear!" gulp in my throat.

"Let me get you another cup, Mr. President," I said.

"That's okay," he said. "It looks like a tick off Millie [the first dog]."

> "It looks like a tick off Millie."

I figured that when the Kava crystals were mixed with the hot water, all of the crystals hadn't dissolved. When I stirred it a little, foam appeared on the top and I couldn't tell that all of the crystals hadn't dissolved, then one of them had fallen out on the napkin.

While the president was talking to me about it, I could feel the eyes of the senior staff boring a hole right through me. As I felt the heat of the moment rising, the president—the gentleman and class act that he was—made everything okay. You had to be there!

Presidential Horseshoe Tournament

Once, I was talking to one of the president's staff members about the ongoing horseshoe games at the White House, and I made the comment that I was an avid player. The staff member asked if I had made it known to the president, and I said that it would not be appropriate for me to do that.

Horseshoes had been near and dear to my heart since age five. One thing led to another and I commented that I hadn't been beaten in forty-one years. I had always let my horseshoes do the talking and the losers do the walking. You may recall how Muhammad Ali bragged about his boxing prowess for twenty years because he could back it up? Well, that's the way I felt. So the staff member ended up telling President Bush about me.

To Phyllis and John Haigh
With best wishes, Geo Bush

The president later called me into the state room and said, "What's this I hear that you're a horseshoe player?"

"Yes, sir, I've been playing for many years."

He then gave me a personal invitation, telling me to team up with a partner and take part in his tournament. I later received a letter from the office of the president, announcing the President's Fall Classic Invitational Horseshoe Tournament. The letter outlined all the tournament players, and the order in which they would play, and also includes the president's ground rules.

So, on October 12, 1989, my partner and I were scheduled to play the first round against an aide to the president and his partner at 5:30 p.m. We arrived an hour early, excited and ready to go, with my boss—the presidential pilot (our manager)—at our side. We watched the president's son Marvin and granddaughter Marshall practicing. First Lady Barbara Bush, along with Marvin's wife, several aides, and grounds people, stood by, watching. We finally shook hands with our opponents and assumed our positions. The apprehension was there until we threw the first few shoes that found their mark, and then it was all over but the handshaking at the end. We didn't have a fat lady there to sing, but we did say, "Next!"

The president came out to watch as we were ending the second game, which, by the way, was 21–0. The president yelled to us and asked if we would like to play him and Marvin that day instead of waiting until next week for the regular game with them.

John – you're too good! [signature]

"Okay," we said, and then proceeded to shake hands and start.

I was so caught up in the excitement of it all that I didn't keep track of the score, but we did win both games.

"Okay, let's play again," the president said.

So we played again—and again and again … three extra games. They won the third game hands-down playing by his rules. He had already dubbed my partner and me "Mr. Automatic and Mr. Smooth" due to our accuracy of play. Mr. Bush really was a good sport, getting right down in the clay with us to measure points closest to the peg.

During the match, he'd say things like, "Come on, John, put one on so I can top it!"

As we said our good-byes that night, President Bush told me, "You'll like the clay in Alaska this time of the year to play on—on your new assignment. And we better get these guys checked for steroids, and have them do a urinalysis before they leave the grounds."

Everyone laughed, and then President Bush said that he would be back to cheer us on through the next level of eliminations.

We won all of our preliminary matches without any losses, and were ready for the final match. On November 19, 1989, it was the main event at the White House, and was all the participants were there

with their wives and husbands. We arrived at 2:00 p.m. and were met by the president's personal assistant, who escorted us by way of the Oval Office for a quick peek. My wife Phyllis and I were thrilled. From the Oval Office, we proceeded toward the pitching area, where a large banquet table had been set up and filled with hot beverages and snacks. At 2:45, we were invited to watch the president's helicopter landing on the South Lawn. I'd seen it land and park in front of Air Force One many times, but none of that had been quite as impressive as this. The president and first lady got off along with Millie the first dog, and then headed toward the horseshoe pits. Everyone gathered around the pitching area, and the president had all the players get

together for a group photograph before the games began.

The games started between the Groundskeepers and the Uniformed Division, which went the full distance of five games. The Uniformed Division won the consolation games. While we were watching, everyone was getting

To John Haigh
With best wishes, to *a fine man.*

Geo Bush

Barbara & Geo Bush
Chief Master Sgt (Air Force) John Haigh

pretty chilled, and the president offered me his official NFL Dallas Cowboys jacket to wear. I gratefully accepted the jacket, and it felt nice, even for a Pittsburgh Steelers fan.

Next came our turn to play the Ushers Office players, who were wearing sweatshirts with large letters on the front that spelled out "Underdogs" beneath two interlocking horseshoes. They'd also had sweatshirts made up for the president and first lady, which said "Mr. Sixpack" and "Mrs. Sixpack" on the back. The Bushes donned their sweatshirts and said, "Let the games begin."

We assumed our positions and started. I was very strong at first—I say strong in the negative sense, because I was overshooting the peg. Meanwhile, my partner was too short. Needless to say, we lost the first game by a score of 21 to 14. This was our first official loss of the tournament. I humbly changed the score markers back to zero for the second game. Still pitching strongly and overshooting, we were getting hammered to the tune of 17–1. I was feeling pretty low by now because of the bragging I had done. I looked upward with my eyes closed and said, "Lord, you gave me this gift. Would you please help me to use it?"

I blocked everything out of my mind, stepped up, and threw a ringer. My opponent topped mine with a ringer, but then I threw another ringer, topping his, which, according to the president's rules, gave us nine points. Then I threw a series of double-ringers each time. We won the second game by a rousing score of 21–20. So it was one game each.

When I had finally started to throw well, the president yelled, "John's back!"

Amidst a lot of cheering for us and our opponents, along with "oohs" and "aahs," we won the next two games to win the tournament. It was a great moment in our lives when it was over, knowing we had won. The president and first lady got us all together for another group picture, after which they

passed out the winners' gifts. My partner received a golf putter, and a keychain with a medallion in the shape of a horseshoe, with the presidential seal in the center and his name on the back. I was also given a keychain of the same design, along with a limited-edition Toney Penna driver that was red, white, and blue with an eagle embossed on it. I also received a Cross pen set in a wooden case that had "President George Bush, America's No. 1 Patriot, Protecting Our Nation's Flag" inscribed on the outside. This was given to me as the MVP award—a very touching moment.

To John Haigh, horseshoe champ, patriot. friend. Best Wishes Gy Bush

Drug Conference in Colombia

On February 15, 1990, the president made a decision to spend the night aboard Air Force One before departing for the drug conference in Cartagena, Colombia. The primary crew arrived in the wee hours of the morning (or as we say in the flying business, "O dark early"). Due to all the articles in the newspapers and television about threats against the president going to Colombia, I was concerned about my own future and the futures of all my fellow crew members. I was so concerned that I handwrote a last will and testament the morning of departure. I had a fellow coworker witness it, and then I left it in the desk drawer in my office. Being a Christian, and having already talked to the Almighty about placing his shield of security over and around us, I still felt it necessary to write this document for my family.

The flight was uneventful for all four hours and fifteen minutes. We served a full breakfast of orange juice, chilled fruit salad, sausage omelets with cheese sauce, Potatoes O'Brien, croissant, and a choice of beverage. The movies available that day were *Ghostbusters II*, *A Dry White Season*, *Great Balls of Fire*, *Pink Cadillac*, *Star Trek V: The Final Frontier*, and *Lock Up*.

I didn't give much thought about danger until we started our descent into the airport. It looked like we were coming in over jungle terrain. In my mind, I thought about all the different ways a money-hungry, publicity-seeking terrorist could be lurking out there, waiting to make his devastating mark in history—by destroying Air Force One and killing everyone on board. However, it was a graceful descent and smooth landing. A normal VIP arrival ceremony was staged, with remarks given by the president. While he was making remarks, I stood nearby the awaiting Marine One helicopter with his baggage in one hand, my heart in the other, and a lump in my throat, hoping that he would hurry up and get done so that I could stop feeling like a turkey in a turkey shoot! As the presidential party finally boarded the helicopter, I did my thing, scurried back aboard Air Force One, and staaaaaayed there!

We were given security badges to wear in case we wanted to visit the duty-free shop, but we all said, "No thanks!" Before departure that evening, the president made a few more remarks, and then held a brief question-and-answer session with the press. I wanted to get out of there as soon as possible, if not sooner, because of the threats. Finally, as we ascended out over the water, the airplane felt like a flying envelope of excitement, coming from the success of the visit—and the relief from the mounting tension of worry, having wondered if those vicious threats would be carried out. As we climbed higher and higher over the water, away from the danger zone, we could feel the excitement in the air. We joyfully served their choice of beverage, with a nice cold face cloth to cool their heated brows. After reaching a safe altitude, we served:

DINNER

Pasta and Fruit Salad
Strips of Barbecue Beef
Parsleyed Whole Potatoes
Fresh Blue Lake Green Beans
Dinner Roll
Succulent Peach Pie
w/ Whipped Cream
Choice of Beverage

Air Force One

Then came their favorite after-dinner aperitif. The arrival at Andrews Air Force Base was jubilant for everyone. I felt even more relieved than when I had gone to Moscow for the first time and returned home. But an example of how some people react to these type of situations came when I walked over to the press camera pit area to express how good it felt to be home safe and sound. The faceless person behind the camera yelled back at me, saying, "I couldn't care less. I get paid by the hour to be here."

A Visit with Former President Reagan

We made a special trip to Los Angeles so that President Bush could pay a visit to former President Ronald Reagan. The flight crew had also been given a special invitation to see our former commander in chief.

During our three-hour visit, Mr. Reagan shared many stories with us, and he seemed to enjoy it as much as we did, even taking photos with each of us.

One of President Reagan's closest friends, Mr. A. C. Lyles, invited us to visit his office at Paramount Studios. His office was wall-to-wall pictures, a veritable "who's who" of movie stars that went back to the silent-film days. Mr. Lyles told us that he had been best man when President and Mrs. Reagan were married. He also mentioned that he, Mr. Reagan, and James Cagney had been buddies in their younger days.

That same afternoon, we were taken to see the TV sets for *Cheers* and the original *Star Trek* series, where we each took a turn sitting in Captain Kirk's command chair. We also took a group photo in front of the transporter pad where they would "beam up" crew members on the show. Down the hallway from there was the office of the late Gene Roddenberry, the creator and producer of *Star Trek*.

That evening, we had a special treat: going to the Magic Castle, where past and present members ranged from Johnny Carson to Houdini. The manager told us that anytime we came to the Magic Castle, we could just say "Air Force One" as the magic password to get in (being recommended

To CMSgt John Haigh
With best wishes, Ronald Reagan

by A. C. Lyles probably didn't hurt, either).

Our final tour stop was Universal Studios, where we saw the house from *Psycho*, the shark from *Jaws*, and the area where Charlton Heston as Moses parted the Red Sea in the *Ten Commandments*. We also visited the set where the kids had flown through the air on their bicycles in the movie *E.T.* What a trip—what a privilege!

Kennebunkport: July 1990

The Fourth of July, 1990, was a historic day for the country and the US Coast Guard. The Air Force One crew had been invited to attend the fireworks celebration in Kennebunkport, Maine. Little did we know that once we arrived there, we would be transported by the Coast Guard on a small cutter out to the Coast Guard's finest ship, the USS *Eagle*—a sailing ship formerly owned by the Germans in 1936 before becoming US property after the war. The ship measured 295 feet long and was powered by three humongous sails. The ship served as the training vessel for the Coast Guard Academy cadets. I had the chance to talk to Admiral Kime, the Coast Guard commandant at the time, and he told me that he had trained aboard the *Eagle* in the late 1950s.

We boarded the *Eagle* about an hour before the Bush family. The cutters that came after us brought the White House staff, family members, and guests from Kennebunkport. The president arrived driving his speedboat, *The Fidelity*. He and the first lady, along with several members of the Air Force One flight crew, then boarded the *Eagle*. Watching everyone board the ship was exciting, especially considering they had to hit just the right moment to go aboard. The *Eagle* was moving back and forth with the waves of the ocean, and the much smaller cutters bounced up and down, back and forth. Finally the president and first lady were piped aboard, continuing the special "piping aboard" sounding call for the arrival of the captain and senior officers on deck.

The Zambellis (the first family of fireworks, from New Castle, Pennsylvania) oversaw the fireworks that evening. The fireworks were set off from a nearby barge, a short distance away from Walker's Point, and the fireworks were indeed a sight to see—and even more exciting from our position on the *Eagle*.

A once-in-a-lifetime experience, and made even more memorable by the president making the rounds, shaking hands, and taking pictures.

Kennebunkport: August 1990

Later that summer, we departed Washington for the First Family's summer vacation in Kennebunkport. I had been pondering all the earth-shaking news taking place, as all of the world governments were actively expressing their rebuttal of the Iraqi invasion of Kuwait. As I was standing in the state room of Air Force One awaiting the arrival of Marine One, I thought to myself, *This has to be a most trying time for my commander in chief: to be maintaining a balance of thought between world events taking place, and carrying these affairs on his shoulders to*

...This has to be a most trying time for my commander in chief...

Kennebunkport, with hopes for a bit of peace and quiet, while at the same time, our comrades in arms are maintaining a peaceful but defensive vigil on the borders of Saudi Arabia and Kuwait.

As the president boarded the aircraft, he appeared to be up, refreshed, and confident, shaking my hand and saying, "Good to see you." He knew I had taken several weeks' vacation, and he asked what we did, where we went, etc. I shared a little about our annual family trip to the oldest amusement park in the country: Kennywood Park, near Pittsburgh, Pennsylvania. I also shared about my time on the golf course and what I figured would be my best game of golf for life. He interrupted me and said, "I have something for you." With that, he lifted his briefcase into his lap, opened it, and handed me a sleeve of golf balls from Disney World. Then he said he wasn't too sure how well they would play. He didn't know that I couldn't tell the difference between the best or the worst golf balls in the game. I have always just loved to play, and whatever happens, happens. I used to make the comment that if I could play golf like I pitch horseshoes, move over Arnie and Jack and make room for me! Ha-ha!

The president held an on-board press conference, and we offered lunch to those who didn't have a chance to eat at the White House. We served them a shaved turkey sandwich with Swiss cheese on pumpernickel bread, plus chips and relishes, and they enjoyed it. Upon arrival at Pease Air Force Base, New Hampshire, the usual crowd of well-wishers was there to greet us. We went down ahead of the First Family, carrying their bags to be loaded on Marine One. We usually stand off to the side between the helicopter and Air Force One while the First Family was escorted to the chopper. The president was doing his normal hand-waving to the crowd, but then he looked toward me, pointed a hand, and made a golf-swinging gesture, smiling, already knowing that we would be playing golf, weather permitting. This sentiment went hand in hand with the Fourth of July trip, when he wrote me a personal note to be given to the golf pro at the course he played in Kennebunkport. The note said, "Ken, please let John and his friends use my clubs to play." That was nice! President Bush was a kind and gentle person who loved his family, his friends, his country, his job, and those of us who served him personally. I cherished those moments, as I know he did. I supported him during those trying times in history, as well as during the good times. The world was waiting to see what would take place in the Middle East, as we stood by, ready to serve our country.

First Trip on New Air Force One

On Sept. 6, 1990, President Bush boarded the new 747 that would serve as Air Force One. He was met on board by his pilot, Colonel Danny Barr. After talking with the president, Colonel Barr returned to his crew position, and I escorted the president on his first tour of the new plane shortly before takeoff. He visited each compartment,  asking questions and making comments about the size and beauty of this great new symbol of the presidency. One of his comments was, "It's marvelous in every way. The latest in technology, certainly, and very, very comfortable. It is magnificent." Someone asked him whether he might soon test the in-air refueling capability on a long day trip, say, to the Persian Gulf. He smiled and said, "Stay tuned. Have plane, will travel." He then said that he'd visited the cockpit area, but he would not try to fly the plane, even with his Navy pilot training. "A little sitting there, maybe," he said, "but I wouldn't understand how to start this thing." Someone also teased him about wearing his seatbelt at his desk, and he said, "It's my pilot training: I always wear a seatbelt for takeoff and landing."

Shortly after leveling off in flight, which took a bit longer than the old 707, the members of the White House press pool were brought forward by an assistant to the president to tour the aircraft. During their state room visit, they mentioned to the president that he had done well for himself with the new aircraft, and he quickly corrected them: "Thank heavens somebody else did okay for me five years ago [meaning President Reagan]." He told them that Congress had approved the purchase in 1986 under the previous administration. They asked if he would do anything to personalize the plane, and he said, "Nothing. It's beautifully done. It doesn't need anything else. We might hang some pictures." The president's chief of staff, John Sununu, added, "We did ask for piranhas in the sinks back in the press area."

To John Haigh
with best wishes,
Gen Bush

Personal Tour of Air Force One

Since I can't take you on a tour of the plane we flew back then, please let me take you through the aircraft via your imagination. After being cleared through security and granted access by the presidential pilot, you would be escorted through the aircraft by a member of the Air Force One flight crew—one crew member for every two visitors. You would enter the aircraft through the forward passenger door, then make an immediate left to see the accommodations for the president, which included an executive suite consisting of a state room with dressing room, lavatory/shower, and the president's office. Next would be the medical annex, which was outfitted with medical equipment and supplies for minor medical emergencies. The forward galley would come next, and that area provided service for up to fifty passengers, including the flight crew. Food was prepared according to the likes of the First Family, which might have included anything from hot dogs to beef Wellington. The only items we could not prepare on board were deep-fried foods.

The next compartment was for the senior staff, such as the press secretary, national security advisor, chief of staff, and cabinet secretaries, if they are on board. Continuing down the aisle, you would come to the conference/dining room, where the president held high-level staff meetings or going-away parties for members of his staff.

The next compartment was for the administrative staff, such as the president's personal secretary, personal physician, speechwriters, director of the White House Military Office, and the military aide (the person who carried the nuclear football). The next compartment was the computer room, with the latest state-of-the-art computers, fax machines, etc.

The next compartment you would come to was for the president's guests. Whenever a member of Congress or the Senate from the president's party was running for reelection, that person would be invited aboard and seated in the guest area. Whenever the aircraft arrived at the destination of that politician, the president would invite that person to deplane with him for a photo opportunity.

The next compartment was for the Secret Service detail. They were strategically located just forward of the White House press, to make sure that no one from the press could go forward without the express approval of a White House staff member or the president. The last compartment was the rear galley, which could also serve up to fifty passengers.

In total, the main deck of the plane had six lavatories and eighty-five telephones, plus a television in each compartment. The flight crew was located in the upper deck, which was outfitted with bunks, a lavatory, and mini galley.

The lower rear compartment had its own self-contained baggage loader and rear stairs. The front lower compartment had stairs, refrigeration and freezer units, and a dry storage area. As mentioned earlier, the aircraft also had in-flight refueling capability.

The length of the aircraft was 231 feet, 10 inches, and the height 63 feet, 5 inches. It had a wingspan of 195 feet, 8 inches, and it traveled at a speed of 701 miles per hour, at a ceiling of 45,100 feet. Maximum takeoff weight was 833,000 pounds, with a range of 9,600 statute miles (8,348 nautical miles) with a crew of twenty-six personnel. The president had a primary 747 and a backup, which was outfitted exactly the same. The color scheme throughout each aircraft was a desert motif.

The aircraft had the capability of storing up to 2,000 meals for a two-week trip around the world. The only items that needed to be bought ahead of time were perishable items such as fruits and fresh vegetables. The plane had the capability of freezing electrically, or dry ice, in case of a loss of power. Whenever Air Force One was alerted for a mission with the president, the flight attendants went shopping in civilian clothes and only purchased food from sources preapproved by the Secret Service. They also varied the routes taken to the grocery stores for security purposes.

The aircraft had the capability of storing up to 2,000 meals...

When your tour would come to an end, you would receive a souvenir packet, which included a picture of the airplane, a box of M&M's with the president's signature, several books of matches with the presidential seal, a cocktail napkin with presidential seal, all as a small token to remember your visit. I liked to say that it was a small return on your tax dollar—well-spent.

"May I Take a Picture?"

Ambassador Joseph Verner Reed, long-time personal friend of the president, was selected as the chief of protocol of the United States of America. The ambassador was our official VIP on a return trip from Europe with the president, flying aboard the backup aircraft. He was a genuinely nice, personable, well-dressed gentleman (to the nines, as some would say) of the highest esteem. When you met him, he made you feel like you were the most important person in the world at that moment. He was tall, slender, refined, articulate, and well-suited for his position.

Shortly before arriving at Andrew Air Force Base, Mr. Reed made a request to the flight attendant, asking if it would be all right to take a picture in his compartment. The flight attendant got the okay from the aircraft commander. So, as all the passengers were deplaning, they noticed the ambassador leaving the aircraft with a large framed picture under his arm: a photo of the First Family, which had been hanging in his compartment. The crew thought that he wanted to take a photograph with his camera, instead of actually removing a picture off the wall and taking it!

...Mr. Reed made a request to the flight attendant...

Campaigns

It was the first day of the final campaign for the 1990 congressional, senatorial, gubernatorial, and local political futures. The president was in the middle of problems in the Middle East with Saddam Hussein, the budget game between the House and Senate opponents on the Hill, and all those who wanted to protect their own special interests instead of doing what was right for the country. The president was only one person with the security interest of the country as his primary agenda, not providing a job for every citizen. The majority voice of Congress was the real tuning fork in curing our economic ills. That meant curbing spending regardless of who it affected: make the rich, middle, and poor classes pay their fair share for taxes. I'd heard it said that each person who worked should pay a flat 10 percent of their income for taxes. So if you made a million dollars a year, you would pay $100,000 in taxes, with no loopholes. If you made $10,000 a year, you would pay $1,000 in taxes, with no loopholes. In general, people have not minded paying taxes, as long as it's been fair. To me, it's always been just like the draft: no one should be exempt from serving our country in time of war. A loss of life is real: rich or poor. Thus, the people should speak with their vote.

When the president arrived at the aircraft, he looked at me and said, "John, I suffered a terrible loss to the Housemen at the White House horseshoe pits." We also discussed my defeat later on in flight. I told the president that I had done a little research to find the right words that might be appropriate for defining our defeat, and I said, "Mr. President, in the game of life, it's good to suffer a few losses in the early stages, in order to eliminate the worry of maintaining an undefeated season." He laughed and said, "That sounds like something my aide would say."

We left sunny California and the political dogfight there, heading for the cool, windy city of Albuquerque, New Mexico, where an airport rally awaited us. Then, on the way to Houston, we somehow got back on to one of the president's favorite subjects: horseshoes. He told me privately that he was impressed with the way I pitched.

Returning from Houston on election day, we served Texas BBQ, and everyone was looking forward to returning home after a grueling campaign finish. The president talked with his personal aide and me about the final horseshoe match scheduled for Monday, Nov. 12, at 3:45 p.m. He said he would like to have me as his partner, and that he wanted to take on all comers after the final match. He made several comments to me as we were taxiing into the arrival area at Andrews about life, saying, "Remember where you heard this: 65 percent of life is showing up; the rest is getting on with it. And number two: your worst day on the golf course is better than your best day at the office."

I agreed, of course, and said, "I'm going to use that one, Mr. President."

Operation Desert Shield

In November 1990, we departed Andrews Air Force Base at 6:45 p.m. on the first leg of our historic flight to Prague, Czechoslovakia. The president and first lady went to bed shortly after takeoff, while we served prime rib dinner to the rest of the staff and party, accompanied by the *piece de resistance* for dessert: the Kentucky Derby delight named "Louisville Lust." The flight last just over eight hours, so we arrived at 9:00 a.m. local time, 3:00 a.m. Washington time. We were welcomed by a twenty-one-gun salute upon arrival. Heading up the welcoming committee was our ambassador to protocol, the "Master of the Grand Gesture" himself, the Honorable Joseph Verner Reed, along with the president of Czechoslovakia, Vaclav Havel, and his wife. It was cool and very windy as the two countries' anthems were played. The president trooped the line, inspected the troops, and then the motorcade departed.

On Nov. 18, 1990, we departed Prague for an interim stop at Ramstein Air Force Base, Germany, where we received a rousing welcome by the American troops and their families. The president visited Chancellor Helmut Kohl, receiving his full support for our Operation Desert Shield in the Middle East. As we departed from there, the same crowd came out to see us off. The president and first lady stood at the top of the steps, gave a thumbs-up, then waved to the crowd. Both of them were visibly moved by the response, as it showed support for our troops in Saudi Arabia.

"...this aggression will not stand."

In regards to the situation in Kuwait, the president had recently said, "I am as determined as I have ever been that this aggression will not stand. If an embargo would force the American people to withdraw from Hawaii, then Iraq would consider withdrawal from Kuwait."

On the way to the Middle East, the president was reading the Bible, and I made a comment to him that I appreciated seeing him do that.

"Are you into reading the Word?" he asked me.

"Mr. President, I don't leave home without it," I said.

The president had made another announcement to the press that, "This [the US conflict in the Middle East] will not be another Vietnam." I agreed, having been in the military during those perilous times and knowing that we did not have a defined purpose for being there.

During our stop in Jiddah, Saudi Arabia, General "Stormin'" Norman Schwarzkopf—the commanding general of all the Desert Shield troops—joined us and had lunch with the president while we prepared for the next stop in Saudi Arabia, where he would visit with the troops in the field. He and the first lady had a great visit with the troops and were elated when they returned to the aircraft.

The Persian Gulf buildup was in progress—with our personnel doing everything possible to handle the 430,000 Iraqi soldiers, 3,500 tanks, and 2,200 artillery pieces that the Iraqi army had in Kuwait and southern Iraq. It was believed that the air superiority of the US forces would prevail, no matter what Saddam Hussein had in place. It was great to have the support of most of our allies, with a UN resolution that gave our president what he needed to remove this insane dictator from Kuwait City.

Operation Desert Storm

On Jan. 16, 1991, President Bush told the nation that he ordered airstrikes to destroy all of the Iraqi's ability to wage war—and not just to push them out of Kuwait.

"We are determined to knock out Saddam Hussein's nuclear bomb potential," he said. "We will also destroy his chemical weapon facilities. Much of Saddam's artillery and tanks will be destroyed. We will not fail."

He also promised to bring troops home at the earliest possible moment after the fighting ends. The fight soon ended in one of the most successful, strategically fought battles, and we had removed Saddam's troops from Kuwait City. After the battle was over, and it was safe for the president to travel to the Middle East, President and First Lady Bush returned to personally thank the troops for the successful completion of Desert Storm.

Some people made comments that we should have continued on into Baghdad and taken out Saddam. But the UN resolution didn't call for that. We were only empowered to remove Saddam and his troops from Kuwait

City, and then it was over. Personally I believe that the only reason the UN agreed with this resolution was because the French, Germans, and especially Russians were on the dole financially from Saddam. They were providing goods and services to Iraq, including arms, and were getting rich as a result. To take Saddam out would have been devastating to their financial gains in the future.

I also believe that if the presidential election would have been held at that time, President Bush would have been reelected by a landslide based on his leadership in this time of crisis.

Economic Summit: London

The First Family spent three days at their Kennebunkport estate, preparing for our trip to France, London, Greece, and Turkey, all from July 11–22, 1991. During his stay in Kennebunkport, President Bush played a record eighteen holes of golf in one hour and twenty-one minutes at the Cape Arundel Course—better known as aerobics golf.

After departing for Paris, the president and first lady went to bed, and were later awakened to have breakfast before our arrival and his meeting with President Francois Mitterrand.

From Paris, we were off to London, where the leaders of the world would meet for an economic summit. Colonel Barr—the pilot—and I were alerted to report to the aircraft for a show-and-tell for some very special guests: Prince William (then age nine) and his brother Prince Harry (age six). Soon they arrived, escorted by their security man, named Trevor. They got out of their vehicle, extended their hands, and said, "How do you do?" like young gentlemen. The boys were dressed in dark blue blazers, gray ties, white shirts, and loafer-style shoes, and were attentive to requests from Trevor.

We boarded the aircraft and took them to the bedroom suite first. Young Harry was sitting on the president's bed when all of a sudden another aircraft taxied by, making a lot of noise. Harry looked at me real seriously and then asked, "Are we tyking [taking] off?" I loved his accent!

The princes later saw a candy tray and asked for strawberry-flavored Starbursts, and we let them help themselves. Trevor said, "Boys, what do you say?" They both said, "Thank you very, very, very much!" Then when they asked for more, Trevor said, "Don't eat too much candy. You know the nanny [Olga] will be upset if you're not hungry for lunch."

Then we took them to the upper-deck crew compartment, and when they saw the crew bunks, they got into them and lay there as though they were sleeping, having a good time, like typical young kids. Later, we made a comment about putting a commemorative plaque on the crew bunk, stating that the future king of England lay there.

I mentioned to Trevor before they left that Queen Elizabeth II liked the Velamints during her trip with us, so we gave him a package to take with them.

From there, we went to Athens, Greece, which was extremely hot. The food was great, but I got a bug of some kind and was sick for a few days. The president visited Souda Bay, lasted visited by a US president when Mr. Eisenhower stopped there.

From there, going back to Ankara, Turkey, brought back many memories for me. We were met by the Turkish president, Turgut Ozal. During this visit, the primary crew played a softball game against the backup crew. We later all went out to Cheap Charlie's Brass Shop, where I saw items just like the ones I had already packed away in my

We were met by the Turkish president, Turgut Ozal.

garage, so I had no need to buy any brass. In fact, I figured I might have to increase my prices at my next garage sale.

From Ankara, we went to Instanbul, with President Ozal and his wife as our guests. We served everyone a continental breakfast, and then passed around a birthday card for everyone to sign, including President Bush and President Ozal, in honor of the president's pilot, Colonel Danny Barr.

I took a special liking to President Ozal because he was short, gray-haired, pleasantly plump, wore glasses, had a friendly smile, wore suspenders, had clothes that fit well, and wore a finely trimmed mustache—a very dapper-looking gentleman. I wanted to say *"Mehraba abi"* ("Hello, brother," in Turkish) to the president, but I chose not to because I was afraid he would say more than I would understand and leave me standing there with my mouth open, not knowing what to say next.

"Mehraba abi."

Istanbul was our last stop, and there we stayed in a beautiful hotel overlooking the Bosphorus Strait. The food was great, but some of us even went to the McDonald's there before some sightseeing.

We served lunch and dinner on an eleven-hour flight home, after which the president and first lady thanked us for another job well done.

Trip to Pittsburgh and Nashville

In October 1991, I was excited about the president's trip to western Pennsylvania, where I hail from and had spent most of my life as an avid Pittsburgh Steelers fan. Our guests were Senator Arlen Specter, Congressman Rick Santorum, Congressman Tom Ridge, and former Pennsylvania Governor Richard Thornburgh (the US attorney general at that time) and his wife Ginny.

The flight to Pittsburgh was only fifty minutes, during which time we served lunch:

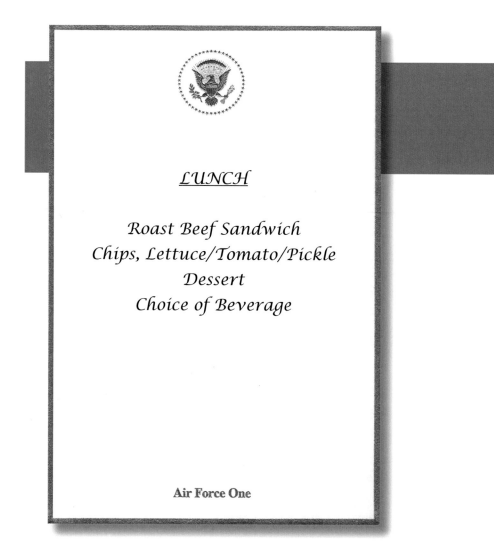

LUNCH

Roast Beef Sandwich
Chips, Lettuce/Tomato/Pickle
Dessert
Choice of Beverage

Air Force One

As the president's guests were deplaning, Congressman Ridge made the comment to me that he would be running for governor of Pennsylvania in the future. Another item of note: one of the people in the receiving line was well-known Pittsburgh philanthropist Elsie Hillman.

We departed Pittsburgh for Nashville. During the nearly two-hour flight, we served snacks and beverages. In Nashville, city officials and representatives from the Grand Ole Opry met us. The president attended the twenty-fifth presentation of the CMA Awards on Oct. 2, 1991. It was a grand event for country music lovers. The president was an avid fan, and we had a lot of country music aboard Air Force One for his listening pleasure.

I was given a copy of the CMA Awards magazine, and on Page 33 was a picture of Travis Tritt. Below the picture was a 25-cent piece, with a caption underneath: "Here's a quarter," referring to Tritt's hit single "Here's a Quarter (Call Someone Who Cares)."

Opening Day at the Reagan Library

It was an early morning departure out of Andrews for the five-hour flight to Point Mugu Naval Air Station in Oxnard, California, to celebrate the opening of the Reagan Library. Those of us who had flown with President Reagan were invited to ride along in the motorcade to the official ceremony.

Opening Day at the Ronald Reagan Presidential Library
November 4, 1991

Shortly after arrival at Point Mugu, we had to leave the aircraft and join the motorcade for the fifty-minute ride to the Reagan Library in Simi Valley.

At least 5,000 people were in attendance, including celebrities such as Charlton Heston, Lee Greenwood, Merv Griffin, and many others. Five presidents and six first ladies attended the event. President Carter made a comment about being the only Democrat present. Out of all the speakers in attendance, the only one who spoke extemporaneously without notes was President Nixon. However, each president made eloquent remarks.

Philadelphia

The flight to the City of Brotherly Love was a short fifty minutes from Andrews, and we served pastries and juice while carrying Senator Specter and some congressmen as guests of the president. All of them were running for reelection.

After deplaning, the president addressed the crowd on a speaker system at the limousine. All of a sudden, he looked up at me at the aircraft doorway and said, "John, make sure these people see the aircraft. Give them a good show-and-tell." I saluted back, and the president and first lady waved from inside the limo.

Our tour guests included seventeen Points of Light representatives (a special program of President Bush) and a minister from the inner-city ghetto area (he was part of a program serving up to 7,000 people, including the homeless). One of our visitors was disabled and walking with a cane. He seemed very excited, but couldn't speak well, yet he still seemed to understand everything I said as he held onto me while walking slowly. After helping him off the aircraft, I said a "thank you" to the Lord for the experience.

> "John, make sure these people see the aircraft."

Ohio, New York, and Maine

We made an eighty-minute flight to Cleveland-Hopkins International Airport in Cleveland, Ohio, where we were met by Governor Voinovich, Major White, and many other dignitaries. The president gave a campaign speech at the Stouffer Tower City Plaza Hotel, focusing on bringing hope and opportunity, encouraging people to think anew and act anew. He talked about how to handle criminals through a program called "Weed and Seed." First, he said you had to "weed out" the gang leaders, drug dealers, and career criminals, and then "seed" the community with expanded employment, educational, and social services—to rebuild the cities through enterprise zones, not government-made work but real jobs in real businesses. He said that "The government may be able to make good laws, but it's never been able to make men good. That doesn't come from Big Brother. It comes from Mother and Father and family. I'm talking the moral sense that must guide us all. In the simplest terms, I'm talking about knowing what's wrong and doing what's right."

> *The government may be able to make good laws, but it's never been able to make men good.*

We departed Cleveland for Westchester County Regional Airport in Westchester, New York, for a fundraising event hosted by the Connecticut state finance chairman. Once there, the chairman introduced the Oak Ridge Boys, who proceeded to sing the National Anthem. The president gave his remarks and then proceeded off stage to participate in a horseshoe pitching event. Before we left, the Oak Ridge Boys performed their finale, singing "American Made."

Then we headed for Sanford Municipal Airport in Sanford, Maine, where the president spent the next few days relaxing, playing golf with Arnold Palmer, boating, and fishing.

On our return to Washington, we had Arnold Palmer's wife—Mrs. Winifred Palmer—as our guest. The president asked me to give her a show-and-tell of the aircraft, and she made the comment to me, "Arnie's going to be so jealous when he hears about this." Arnie apparently had to fly his own aircraft to Washington.

My Last Overseas Trip

My last overseas trip took me to Panama City, Panama, and then on to Rio de Janeiro, Brazil, for the United Nations Conference on Environment and Development. The president and party stayed at the beautiful Sheraton Rio Hotel, while the crew's accommodations were at the Sao Conrado Palace Hotel.

We dined at the Le Coin Restaurant that was recommended by the American Consulate. For $10.00 a person, we each had a meal consisting of filet mignon (the size of a US football) covered with a cheese sauce, and homemade potato chips on the side. We had been advised to go as a group due to various incidents that had taken place involving Americans, including a situation in which an American crew member decided to get his shoes shined by a street vendor. After agreeing on a price, the kid proceeded to start shining his shoes. About halfway through, the kid asked for more money. When the American argued against it, the kid slashed his Achilles tendon with a straight razor. That got our attention—big time!

I had been privileged to stay in many fine hotels around the world, and the one in Rio was one of them, to be sure. However, that was the first time in twenty-seven years of flying around the world that I looked over my balcony in the morning and saw army tanks surrounding the hotel. I couldn't get back to the good old USA fast enough!

My Last Trip on Air Force One

My last active-duty trip on Air Force One was to Laguna Beach, California, for a political fundraising trip. Once there, the crew got together and took me out for dinner, and then a walk along the beach. We took a bunch of pictures to commemorate the trip for my retirement album. One the return trip, my last official meal served was:

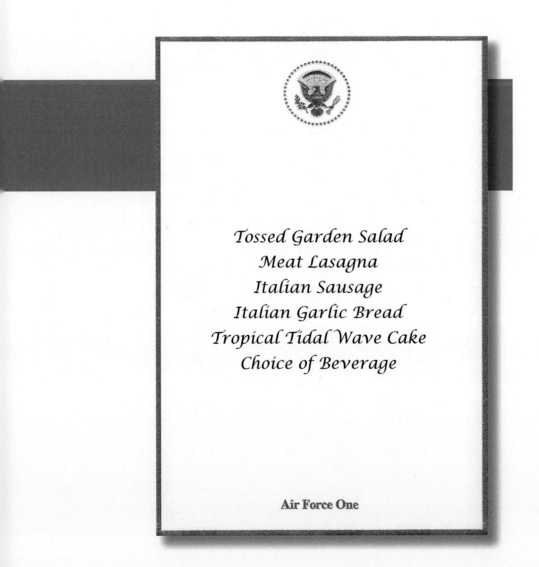

Tossed Garden Salad
Meat Lasagna
Italian Sausage
Italian Garlic Bread
Tropical Tidal Wave Cake
Choice of Beverage

Air Force One

Shortly before arrival at Andrews Air Force Base, my deputy caught me completely off guard with a surprise going-away party in the conference room, with the president, first lady, Colonel Barr, several members of the flight crew, and staff members. The president made a number of comments that humbled me, then they toasted me with champagne. The first lady gave me a big hug, and a number of pictures were taken. Afterward, they sat me down and asked me what my plans were for retirement. I told them that I would like very much to continue working for them at the White House Ushers Office, doing pretty much the same thing there I'd been doing on the aircraft: serving the president and those in his immediate circles.

All business involving the First Family was channeled through the Ushers Office. I told them that I would be personally delivering my resume to the chief usher when we returned to Washington. They wished me well, and Mrs. Bush said, "Don't worry. George will help you."

I thought the celebrating was over—until I walked into the Air Force One kitchen. Out of nowhere came several of my coworkers with about twenty gallons of ice-cold water to pour over my head. I was completely soaked, but very pleased!

Official Photo in Oval Office

Several days after my last trip, I went to the White House for a final visit with the president in the Oval Office. I was amongst other members of the Army, Navy, and Marines who were assigned to the White House Military Office and were either retiring or going on another assignment. When it came my turn to go into the Oval Office, the president was busy shaking hands with some of the others. When he got to me, he looked at me twice with a surprised expression on his face. Then he said, "What are you doing here? Didn't I just see you the other day?" I told him that this was my last official act: having my photograph taken with him. He made a big fuss over me, telling everyone else about my job on the aircraft, winning the horseshoe tournament, and many other nice things. It really made my last visit, and my picture with him, very special.

To CMSgt John Haigh
With best wishes.

Gg Bush

President Bush held many positions in government, such as the chairman of the Republican Party, director of the CIA, member of Congress, first envoy to China, vice president, and finally president. Because he had become known as the "Hands-On President," I was inspired to pen the following in his first year in office:

"THE HANDS-ON PRESIDENT"

It's 1989, our country's in good hands
swearing in our nation's 41st
hails from Maine to Texas, serves from stem to stern
he's George Bush the Hands-On President

Family is his forte, virtue stands out strong
friendship means a lot to him, marked by those along
the way he's chosen serving us, reminds us all again
he's George Bush the Hands-On President

He speaks for right and glory
kindness and gentleness the same
holding on to values helps his claim to fame
patriotism goes real deep, as we remember when
he's George Bush the Hands-On President

Air Force Times Interview and Final Departure

I gave an interview with the folks from the *Air Force Times* newspaper in the Pentagon, and they asked for my departing thoughts on my Air Force career. I told them that I had been personally guided and helped by many top-notch leaders throughout my thirty years of service. They'd taught me to plan my work, then work my plan, and it worked successfully and honorably. I also said that I could pick any ten people from the 89th Military Airlift Wing Special Air Missions to start a business with, and no matter what the business was, we would be successful, primarily due to their can-do attitude. Everyone gave 150 percent of themselves to the customer.

Before departing the Air Force One facility for my last duty day, I went out to the aircraft inside the hangar and walked through each compartment, reflecting on the privileges that had been afforded me for the last thirteen years. I thought about the three men who had occupied the state room in Air Force One during that time, first in the Boeing 707 and then the Boeing 747. They were ordinary men who had reached extraordinary goals in their political careers. I had served as the last chief steward on the Boeing 707, and then the first chief steward on the replacement 747—what an honor. We as Air Force One crew members had served the presidency, not the political party, always keeping in mind to never draw unnecessary attention to ourselves.

...I could pick any ten people from the 89th Military Airlift Wing Special Air Missions to start a business with, and no matter what the business was, we would be successful...

On July 29, 1995, my wife Phyllis was diagnosed with terminal breast cancer at Walter Reed Medical Center. She was restricted to our home with the help of hospice until she died on October 9, 1995.

I received a very special letter from former President Bush that said the following:

Dear John,

Barbara and I just learned the sad news about your Phyllis. We know how hurt and devastated you and your kids must be that this wonderful lady is no longer there in your loving family.

Time will help some, I'm sure of that. Friends will help, and faith will help a lot.

We Bushes are thinking of you, and send our most sincere condolences.

Sincerely,
(Signed by President Bush)

John – I was on AF1 to Israel. But I missed you. Good luck. (This last line was handwritten by him, and then signed again)

I had flown my last flight with President Bush in June 1992, so my family and I were deeply touched by his kind letter.

CHAPTER 5

LIFE AFTER AIR FORCE ONE

Last Official Flight of Boeing 707 Aircraft 27000

In August 2001, the last official flight of the Boeing 707, tail number 27000—the Air Force One for seven sitting presidents—departed Andrews Air Force Base heading to Waco, Texas. Aboard were former Air Force One crew members that had flown for presidents as far back as President Eisenhower through President George W. Bush. On the way to Waco and then on to San Antonio, we all reminisced and told our "war stories" about the many presidents each of us had flown with, plus we recalled the many staff members that supported them, the places we had been, and our personal experiences.

We expected Waco to be scorching hot, but it wasn't. Folks had been praying for rain for quite a while, and rain they'd finally gotten. The next day, President George W. Bush and his staff traveled aboard the Boeing 707 for the last official flight of a sitting president, from Waco to San Antonio. We arrived there and it was raining too hard to have a ceremony. We waited for several hours and the decision was made to fly back to Waco for the ceremony. We arrived there about forty-five minutes before the president and were waiting in our pre-positioned places around the podium. The advance personnel had placed tape for each of us to stand on, thus creating a half-moon-shaped area around the podium. Before taking our places, the security folks checked us with magnetometers for clearance to be near the president. They told us that we couldn't turn our backs to the camera, but to turn sort of sideways and observe as the president and first lady deplaned and headed toward us.

As President and Mrs. Bush neared the podium, we pivoted and turned as they walked by. Along the way, the president and first lady greeted each of us, then we were told to get in closer around the president as he stepped up to the podium. We were so close to him that I could read his speech as he was giving it. His speech was concise and well-read, about ten minutes long. When he finished, he turned and thanked each of us for being there, and for our service to the presidency as Air Force One crew members. I was surprised that he was taller than I'd expected. He looked to be around six feet tall. Of course, at my height, most people are taller than me. As he was departing, he made a passing comment to the press that he would see everyone back at the nation's capital.

We returned to Aircraft 27000, flew back to San Antonio, stayed the night, and departed the next day for Washington. I felt humbled that I had flown on that historic aircraft for eleven years. It had been said amongst us that an airplane that looked so good shouldn't have worked us so hard. But we considered it to be the most beautiful airplane in the world.

Final Flight of Aircraft 27000

In my career, I've had many privileged experiences, but that the final flight of Aircraft 27000 will be forever burned in my memory. When we returned to Andrews, we asked to be part of the final flight. It was well worth the asking. We checked through the passenger terminal at Andrews, and as we were walking toward Aircraft 27000, which was parked in the same location it had been for all the presidents, we could hear Lee Greenwood singing "God Bless the USA."

The press area was set up for the departure remarks by Secretary of the Air Force Dr. James Roche. We were interviewed by various local and national news people before departure, asking us about our experiences as crew members. We boarded the aircraft as official passengers with assigned seats. We found a gift bag on each of our seats, with the great seal on the side and the words "Ronald Reagan Presidential Library, Simi Valley, California." Inside was a light blue hat from the library gift shop. The hat featured two black horses and a white horse, and the words "Reagan Country" embroidered under them. The gift bag also contained a box of Jelly Belly jelly beans (President Reagan's favorite), a video entitled *The Unfinished Work*, and a schedule of events with a picture of Aircraft 27000 on the front.

On board was a congressional delegation, leaders of the Air Force, and former Air Force One crew members. It was a beautiful day for flying, and we were on a similar path that had been taken when President Nixon made his final flight to California. We were served a breakfast consisting of:

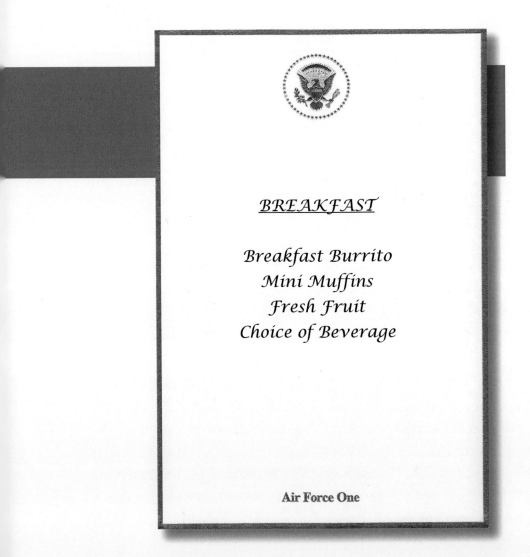

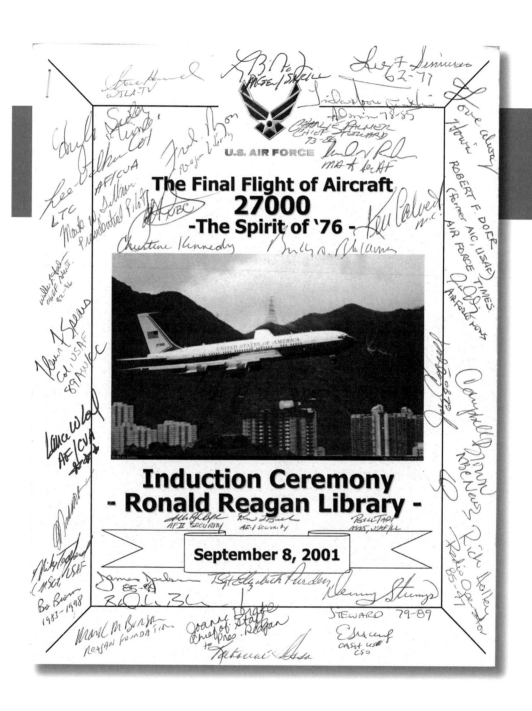

The Final Flight of Aircraft
27000
-The Spirit of '76 -

Induction Ceremony
- Ronald Reagan Library -

September 8, 2001

The service was Air Force One all the way, as usual. Eleven years prior, I had hired the young man in charge of the flight attendants on this trip. Although he may have been young compared to us veterans, his performance, along with his associates, was top drawer.

During the flight, the secretary of the Air Force invited all former crew members to join him in the state room, where he presented each of us with a medallion. We then gathered around the secretary, holding our medallions, for a group photo. Then came another moment to remember. The secretary invited each of us to sit in the world's most powerful airborne seat, where seven sitting presidents had sat. I shared the facts about being on the first and last trip with President and Mrs. Reagan, saying good-bye to them in this state room. By the time they took my picture, I was getting a little teary eyed.

The secretary invited each of us to sit in the world's most powerful airborne seat...

Each passenger took their schedule of events and asked each person on board to sign it, so a lot of signing went on. Then they asked questions about our experiences serving the presidency. I shared my feelings about President Carter's trip to see the hostages in Germany, and several stories about President Reagan.

We arrived in San Bernardino International Airport, formerly known as Norton Air Force Base. Mrs. Reagan came aboard and walked through each compartment, thanking everyone for coming. When she arrived at the table where my old boss Charlie Palmer was sitting, she stopped, gave Charlie a well-deserved hug, and started crying. She was so moved to see the man who had taken care of her and the president as chief steward for six years. Charlie was my mentor and good friend, and I'm sure he was glad to see her as well.

After she deplaned, all of us followed suit into a designated area to share in the planned events. The secretary of the Air Force spoke first, then the director of the Reagan Library, and finally Mrs. Reagan, whose words were wonderful. After the aircraft was officially retired, and the aircraft records were presented, we moved to another area inside where a luncheon buffet had been prepared. We had the opportunity to see many of the former staff members and reminisce about our experiences.

After lunch, we were directed out to the flight line where a brand-new Special Air Missions aircraft, a C-32, was waiting to take us back to Washington. I made a special effort to talk to one of the flight attendants and ask him if he liked his job. His response was, "I love my job." That's what I wanted to hear, because that's the way I'd always felt. It felt good to know that the future of the Air Force One flight attendants would lie in the attitude and performance of people like that.

Invitation to Reagan Library

On Aug. 6, 2002, I received a letter from the chief of staff of the Ronald Reagan Presidential Foundation in Simi Valley, California, thanking me for agreeing to participate in an Air Force One meeting later that month. We soon received our package of instructions, with an airline ticket and hotel reservations inside. On August 18, the former Air Force One pilot, Colonel Bob Ruddick; former chief steward, Charlie Palmer; and I departed for California out of Baltimore-Washington International Airport with an en-route stop at O'Hare Airport in Chicago. Upon our subsequent arrival in Los Angeles, we were greeted by an excited limousine driver—a staunch Ronald Reagan fan—holding a sign that said "Reagan Foundation." The drive to Simi Valley took about fifty minutes. We arrived at the beautiful Posada Royale Hotel, located less than five minutes from the Reagan Library.

The following morning, we enjoyed an incredible breakfast buffet before departing for the library, arriving there at 8:00 a.m. We rode to the library in the Reagan Foundation van up a long winding hill to No. 40 Presidential Drive, at the top of the rolling Simi hills to a 100-acre site that houses the

Ronald Reagan Foundation and library—and about to display the Air Force One exhibit.

Mr. Mark Burson, executive director of the foundation, met us, along with a very excited staff and other invited guests that included folks involved in the Air Force One storyline, such as the writers for what would become the "Pavilion and Plane Interior Experience," photographers, and a host of others, all helping in the preparation to break ground on the new exhibit.

The schedule included introductions, an explanation of how we got to where we were that day, the storyline of the Air Force One Pavilion and Plane Interior Experience, and an open discussion on information that ranged from pilot, copilot, navigator, flight attendants, all other crew members, and general questions for the entire group. One of the main themes was how each of us felt about our interaction with the president and staff, along with the most memorable missions and moments for each of us.

The question that had the most impact on us was, "What was the most humbling moment—or moments—for each of us?" When it came my turn, I reflected back to the day that my boss, Charlie Palmer, told me that the job was mine, if I still wanted it. Then I mentioned the time that President Reagan asked if he could take the electric razor out of the state room lavatory, and how he told me it ended up not working so well but that he had just enough of a charge to finish shaving (a story I've already told earlier in the book). Then I said that President Reagan went on to tell me about breaking in a new pair of blue jeans by jumping into a pool of water, and how he continued to do the same thing as president. I finished my time by reciting the poem that he had inspired me to write and which I presented to the Reagans on the last flight to California. As I was reciting it, I got rather choked up, remembering how much it meant to me to work for them. One of the ladies sitting across from me said I even made her cry.

It was a tearful, but joyful experience for me to share my poem with them. Everyone clapped and said they enjoyed it very much. They also told me that they would like very much to find the plaque with the poem and display it in the library.

On Tuesday morning, Aug. 20, 2002, we returned to the library for a final session that included defining a strategy that would take the word about the library from the local Simi Valley area to the rest of the country—to create a word picture of sorts that would make someone on the East Coast want to make a special trip to California to the Reagan Library, much like those people who travel from the West to East coast to see the nation's capital. Before the meeting started, we received an inspirational tour of the library from one of the staff members—a dear English woman who had worked for Pan American airlines then became an American citizen, and was now working for the Reagan Foundation. Speaking with her British accent, which was very proper, she led us through the library, starting with an explanation of all the medallions that were presented to President Reagan by the heads of state of all the countries he had visited in eight years. The most interesting one was The Most Honourable Order of the Bath, one of the oldest and most prestigious awards from the queen of England. The one that had been placed around President Reagan's neck looked like a large metal set of ringlets (sort of like a large metal lei). When he received the honor and looked down at it, President Reagan told Her Majesty, "This is very nice. Can I keep it?" This surprised her, as no one had apparently asked before. She said that he could take it with him, but when he died, it would need to be returned to England.

"This is very nice. Can I keep it?"

Then, outside the library's replica Oval Office, we saw a large mosaic of President Reagan. A family in Ohio had made it, put in the back of a pickup truck, packed their bags, and then drove to California to see President Reagan. When they arrived there, a member of security greeted them. They went to the back of the truck, uncovered the picture, and said they weren't leaving until they saw the president to personally give him the mosaic. The guard went to the chief of staff, who in turn talked to the president, and he told him to have them come up to his office. The president was so taken aback by their gesture—that they would take the time to do something like this—that he said, "This is what America is all about." He, of course, insisted that this picture would hang in his office in the library.

As we toured, I walked beside Secret Service Agent Mr. Jerry Parr, an agent who was with President Reagan the day he had been shot by John Hinckley. Mr. Parr had been the one who pushed the president into the limousine and gotten him to Georgetown Hospital. We watched a video that replayed the events of the assassination attempt, and I asked Jerry, "Did it take awhile for you to catch your breath?" He said, "You can say that again!" I felt quite humbled at that moment.

In front of the library stood a large piece of the Berlin Wall for everyone to see and touch—a true reminder of President Reagan's vision that began when he said, "Mr. Gorbachev, tear down this wall!" Just a short distance away was the tomb where he and Nancy would be buried, overlooking the Simi Hills and the ocean in the distance.

With the pending Air Force One pavilion, the plane that President Reagan flew on would also soon sit atop this Simi Valley hilltop, taking its place in history next to the myriad of documents and artifacts in a memorial dedicated to one of America's most beloved presidents.

A brochure about the Air Force One Pavilion stated, "We intend to create a memorable and lasting visual experience that enables every American to walk through this magnificent aircraft and feel its awesome power"—or, to put it simply, they wanted to increase the WOW factor at the museum.

The expansion of the library included the construction of a Presidential Learning Center in addition to the Air Force One exhibit. In the Air Force One Pavilion, which is still there today, visitors can get a glimpse of the huge aircraft's nose as they walk down a large corridor linking the museum with the hangar-sized building at cockpit level. You can walk around a three-quarter circle that surrounds the wings, tail, and much of the fuselage of the 153-foot-long Boeing 707. You enter Air Force One from the front, walking through the historic aircraft that served as a flying White House for seven presidents, from Richard Nixon to George W. Bush. Air Force One, No. 27000, is on permanent loan from the United States Air Force

Museum at Wright-Patterson Air Force Base in Dayton, Ohio. The Reagan Library received the aircraft in large part because President Reagan used it the most, logging 150 flights aboard that plane. On top of that, Mrs. Reagan mentioned that the president had always wanted to give people a chance to see the aircraft up close. "Ronnie would be happy to know it's there for everyone to see," she said.

The aircraft had been christened in 1973, flying President Nixon from the White House to his San Clemente home. It made its final voyage twenty-eight years later from Andrews to San Bernardino.

To transport the plane to the library, workers dismantled the 138,000-pound aircraft in San Bernardino by first taking off its 67-foot-long wings and its tail. Then they disassembled the fuselage into four pieces and placed it all on four trucks for the approximate 100-mile drive to the library.

The exhibit building was constructed first, then the plane was reassembled inside. The aircraft faces a glass wall with a view of the hills and sky, to give visitors the impression that it is taking off, according to the building architect, Daniel Clinger.

Museum officials also placed a Marine One helicopter near Air Force One. The helicopter designated Marine One has ferried presidents from the White House to Air Force One at Andrews Air Force Base, and then back again. They also parked a presidential limousine near the aircraft.

At 243,000 square feet, the Reagan Library is by far the nation's largest presidential library. I encourage you to stop by and visit the Reagan Library if you are in California. It is well worth the trip! You can find out more about it by visiting www.reaganfoundation.org.

To close this section, I'd like to leave you with the following remarks, which are excerpts taken from responses given by Mr. Mark Burson, Executive Director of the Reagan Library, when he was a guest

At 243,000 square feet, the Reagan Library is by far the nation's largest presidential library.

on Air Force One's final flight to California and being interviewed by members of the press:

As a historical landmark, this Air Force One has few peers. Tail Number 27000 flew Richard Nixon home after his resignation from office, Gerald Ford after his ascent to the presidency, Jimmy Carter to Germany to meet our freed hostages upon their release from Iran, and Ronald Reagan to Berlin. Little noted is the role this plane played in America's global brinksmanship that began after World War II, making Tail Number 27000 among the most essential soldiers of the Cold War. President Reagan used this aircraft to attend three diplomatic summits—accelerated the collapse of the Soviet Union and restarted freedom's march across Europe. It may not have been the bargaining table, but the enormous presence of Air Force One—and the American spirit it represents—was surely there to be seen. You could say that is served as a presidential partner, the symbolic mode by which President Reagan brought to bear American resolve in the face of an "Evil Empire."

Now the jet upon which seven different presidents rode—but none more than the 40th President—will be placed on public display at the Reagan Library. So, during this morning's ceremonies, as the greatness and grandeur of Air Force One were recalled, I looked to the days, months, and years ahead, as we all must now as much as ever. For the future is where Air Force One—a resource of presidents and treasure of our country—will, after 445 missions and more than one million miles, embark on a new era of public service and proudly call Ventura County, home.

The Reagan Library Air Force One storyline goes like this: the story of Air Force One, the one we want to tell at the

Ronald Reagan Presidential Library, is not really the story of a plane; it's the story of an American hero. The first thing you'll experience on a visit to the Air Force One Pavilion is an orientation film. It will open with an image of Ronald Reagan at his ranch on his horse as the narrator says: "He is in many ways a 19th century man in love with the values of the Western frontier, but he carried those values further into the future than anyone could have ever imagined." And as President Reagan spurs his horse into a gallop, we cut to an image of Air Force One taking off, a montage of work on the plane, a shot of the plane landing in Berlin, then President Reagan stands before the Brandenburg Gate and says, "Mr. Gorbachev, tear down this wall!"

That's the story—in a few simple, bold images; Air Force One was his horse and he rode to the sound of the guns. He rode to where the problem was, looked the other guy in the eye, and dealt with it. In the process, he reconnected America with its heroic past, its can-do spirit—and gave us the confidence we needed, and some thought we'd lost, to face the future boldly, with imagination and courage.

It would be too simple to say that Ronald Reagan ended the Cold War single-handedly, but it's fair to say of Ronald Reagan, as was said of Washington, that he was the "indispensable man." We celebrate that man and his staggering achievement in this pavilion.

It's not, in the end, a history lesson—it's an object lesson in character, in responsibility ... in those values that we as Americans need now more than ever to meet the challenges confronting us at the dawn of the 21st century.

It's not, in the end, about the past—it's about the future. Because that's what Ronald Reagan's presidency was about. Our future, the future we are living now, with the awesome shadow of nuclear apocalypse lifted, is his legacy to all Americans, and to mankind.

Here at the Reagan Library, visitors young and old, from all over the globe, will be able to board the plane he rode, touch a piece of the wall he sent crashing down, relive history that Ronald Reagan made, and look with him into the limitless future he dared to dream for our world. That is, after all, the American Dream—a future without limits. Help us celebrate it here in the Air Force One Pavilion at the Ronald Reagan Presidential Library.

Mr. Elliott Sluhan, of Elliott Sluhan Productions in Toledo—the gentleman whose company produced *Air Force One: The Planes and the Presidents*, Parts I and II—was commissioned to do the narrative voiceover for the Air Force One pavilion film. He is, and has been, a dear friend of all of us who were privileged to be part of the Air Force One's history.

Grand Opening of the Air Force One Pavilion

We finally received the long-awaited invitation to attend the grand opening of the Air Force One Pavilion from the Ronald Reagan Presidential Foundation, to be held on Oct. 21-22, 2005.

We planned a family vacation to coincide with the grand opening. We flew to Las Vegas for a week and visited with my stepdaughter and bonus grandchildren. On the morning of Oct. 20, I experienced a first in my life: a trip through the Mojave Desert. I'd flown over it many times in my career, but it took on a whole new meaning when you're driving.

We stayed at the beautiful Embassy Suites Mandalay Beach Resort Hotel in Oxnard, California, a first-class facility located on the oceanfront. We left early the next morning for the library. Due to heightened security, we were told to arrive no later than 9:00 a.m. A continental breakfast was served in the Air Force One Pavilion before the ceremony started at

11:00 a.m. I recognized many faces from my eight wonderful years with the Reagan administration, such as former Attorney General Edwin Meese, Deputy Chief of Staff Mike Deaver, military aide Colonel Steve Chealander (a former Thunderbird pilot), and personal secretary Kathy Osborne. One of the famous faces was Merv Griffin, who looked great. Merv had been instrumental in providing a replica of the South Lawn of the White House in the rear of the library.

As we registered, we received a "welcome aboard" pamphlet that showed a picture of Aircraft 27000. Inside the pamphlet was a letter from Mrs. Reagan, reflecting on their flying experiences and how President Reagan dreamed of bringing the airplane to his library. Another page indicated that President Reagan had traveled 661,708 miles aboard Air Force One, visiting twenty-six foreign countries and more than 150 American cities while spreading his convictions through face-to-face diplomacy. The pamphlet also mentioned the last flight of Air Force One 27000, departing Andrews

Air Force Base and going to San Bernardino, California. In California, Mrs. Reagan accepted the aircraft from Secretary of the Air Force James Roche, officially concluding its airborne mission to serve the president of the United States.

From that day, and over the next four years, the Air Force One Pavilion went from an idea on a sketch pad to an undertaking of extraordinary proportions. Every day brought about another exciting challenge: disassembly of 27000 by the Boeing Company, the towing of the airplane in the middle of the night across four freeways between San Bernardino and Simi Valley, the laying of the pavilion's cornerstone amidst a ferocious windstorm, the landing of Marine One on the library's replica White House South Lawn, the rain and firestorms that threatened the plane, the reassembly by the Boeing team, the lifting and mounting of Air Force One on its pedestals, the shipment of the original 100-year-old Ronald Reagan Pub almost 10,000 miles from Ballyporeen, Ireland, and finally, the momentous dedication of the exhibit.

Approximately 750 guests attended, including my wife Jessie. The Air Force One crew members were seated on a second-story level that wrapped around the aircraft.

After the dedication ended, we crew members positioned ourselves in our assigned positions that we had held on the aircraft: Colonel Bob Ruddick and Colonel Danny Barr (pilot and copilot), and Lieutenant Colonel James Jackson (navigator) in the cockpit; Chief Master Sergeant Charlie Palmer (chief steward) in the state room; myself (deputy chief steward and then chief steward) in the senior staff compartment; and Chiefs Howie Franklin and Dennis Stump (flight attendants) in the administrative staff area; and Senior Master Sergeant Linda Franklin (stenographer to the Air Force One pilot).

Then President George W. Bush and First Lady Laura Bush escorted Mrs. Reagan up the steps to the main entrance of the plane, where she cut the ribbon. Charlie Palmer opened the main cabin door and the entourage was greeted by each of us as they visited each compartment. Mrs. Reagan walked up to me and gave me a heartwarming hug and thanked me for my service, and I felt very touched. Then the president, first lady, and Mr. and Mrs. T. Boone Pickens each shook my hand as they passed through (Mr. Pickens had made a generous donation of $10 million to the library the day before its official opening).

After the dedication, we returned to the main floor to our reserved tables for a Reaganesque first-class luncheon presented by the presidential caterers.

On the second day of dedication events, we experienced the "Reagan Roundup: Air Force One Review." We arrived early enough to do a little shopping the in library gift shop and then tour the facility.

The program started at 10:30 a.m., and then we took a break for an excellent buffet luncheon. As I was eating, I happened to look up and was awestruck to see the underbelly of this beautiful white, blue, and gold aircraft. It glistened in the light. The way the aircraft is positioned, it looks like it's taking one last flight.

The Reagan Library itself opened in 1991. New exhibits since then have included a colonnade that connects the existing library and three new theaters with the Air Force One Pavilion. After entering the pavilion, visitors see the Flights of Freedom Gallery, which showcases the twenty-six diplomatic flights President Reagan took from 1981 to 1989, including miles flown per year, plus maps and an interactive kids' game. The dividing wall

UNITED STATES OF AMERICA

AIR FORCE ONE

October 21, 2005

gallery features a replica of a section of the Berlin Wall. The Cold War classroom features displays and a six-minute film recounting the Cold War.

The jetway walkway features wall displays and information kiosks for visitors waiting their turn to board Air Force One. As you approach the aircraft, you can view a continuously running movie showing Pilot Bob Ruddick, Chief Steward Charlie Palmer, and me giving remarks about the president and the mission. In the video, I make remarks about the final flight to California and my plaque presentation, displaying the poem he inspired me to write, and then I recite it for each visitor to hear.

The focus of the pavilion is, of course, the presidential plane, Air Force One, a customized Boeing 707. On the floor beneath the plan, you can see a presidential motorcade that includes President Reagan's 1984 parade limousine, a Secret Service vehicle, and a police cruiser, along with motorcycles. You can also see a 120-foot-by-14-foot mural called "The History of the Flying White House," which depicts twenty-two different planes used in support of presidential flights. Also on the ground floor is a Sikorsky Marine One helicopter used by President Lyndon Johnson.

In her remarks that second day, Mrs. Reagan reminded us of what her husband used to say: "Kennedy has an airport, Johnson has a space center, but I am one lucky man to have a pub named after me in Ireland. Now that's really something."

After the short speech, Mrs. Reagan asked those in the audience to raise their glasses "to Ronnie."

George H. W. Bush Library

In November 2007, at the invitation of President George W. Bush, my wife and I attended the grand re-opening of the George H. W. Bush Presidential Library at Texas A&M University in College Station, Texas. We arrived

the day before the opening ceremony, and the president's pilot, Colonel Danny Barr, and his wife Elaine were there to meet us, and then they showed us around the city. Colonel Barr was a 1968 graduate of Texas A&M. He is also one of the finest pilots that has ever flown an airplane. I'm proud to have worked for him, and to call him my friend.

We arrived at the library early the following day. Sportscaster Jim Nantz, a friend of President George H. W. Bush, served as the emcee. At eleven o'clock, Jim said, "Folks, we have a surprise for you today. Look up."

President George H. W. Bush then surprised everyone by skydiving in tandem with a member of the US Army Golden Knights parachute team to open the ceremony. He remarked later that, "I couldn't see myself sitting around at age eighty-three drooling on myself."

I had an opportunity to speak to the former president and first lady, and they still remembered me even though it had been fifteen years since we had said our good-byes. I can only hope to look half as good as they do at that age.

USS George H. W. Bush Aircraft Carrier

In January 2009, my wife and I had the privilege of attending another ceremony that honored the elder President Bush: the commissioning of the USS *George H. W. Bush* aircraft carrier at Norfolk Naval Air Station in Norfolk, Virginia—the largest naval base in the world. Once again, my old boss Colonel Danny Barr and his wife Elaine were there with us, along with Mrs. Kim Johnson, stenographer to Colonel Barr on Air Force One. It was another joyous occasion to see former staff members and to reminisce about the great times aboard Air Force One.

When you speak of once-in-a-lifetime experiences, my wife and I definitely count this one high on our list. We sat there in awe of this momentous occasion honoring a great man and a great president, one that historians will warmly remember. We even had a front-row seat for this wonderful event, sitting next to a former member of the former president's staff, and she captured the details of this day, which I'd like to share with you here:

> Saturday, January 10, 2009, was one of those days I felt lucky to be alive. It certainly was a day I won't forget: clear blue skies, cold breeze coming across the waters of the Chesapeake Bay to the world's largest navy base, at Norfolk, Virginia. As we walked down the giant pier 14—there can't be too many docks that, like it, can hold 20,000 people—we gaped at the sheer size of the USS *George H. W. Bush*. It's roughly equal to the Empire State Building laid on its side, with a flight deck on top that takes up four and a half acres.
>
> By luck, we got seats in the front row and happened to sit between the former Chief Steward of Air Force One and a builder of the memorial to soldiers and sailors killed in Special Operations. We all told stories and took pictures of each other, figured out friends we had in common, people watched, and smiled and took it all in. Soon enough, the choppers carrying the President and First Lady and former

President and Mrs. Bush landed on the flight deck and the commissioning ceremony began.

After "Hail to the Chief" was played by the Navy Band, we all stood for a 21 gun salute in honor of the President. The other times I'd been present for a 21 gun salute were at military funerals at Arlington National Cemetery. Instead of rifles, though, this time they used anti-aircraft guns aboard the ship. The sound was so loud it made your heart skip. The boom and crackle bounced through the canyons on battleships and destroyers lined up and down the pier. But the effect was the same as when I'd heard it graveside: a piercing sense of your own mortality, of the passing of life, of being a part of something far bigger than yourself. The white smoke from the guns puffed away in the breeze as the crowd watched in silence.

Sailors from the ship comprised a small amateur choir, who sang the National Anthem and colors were presented. The Governor of Virginia spoke briefly, and then Secretary Gates introduced President Bush #43. They both gave great speeches, but the President's was especially good. He talked about his parents' great 64 year love affair, and his feeling that his dad was the best father anyone could ever ask for. "For as long as we live, we will carry with us Dad's other lessons: that integrity and honor are worth more than title or treasure, and that the truest strength came from the gentlest soul."

That pretty much sums up why every one of those 20,000 people were there, because that is what we all love about George Bush. Then former President Bush got up to speak. Betting was heavy among friends that he wouldn't make it through his remarks without choking up, but he did beautifully. No one could have written for him what he said; he's been waiting so long for this day that it was no doubt he penned his own remarks, maybe even years ago. He reminisced about another commissioning ceremony 65 years earlier, for the USS *San Jacinto*. That was the ship he was sent to World War II on, and that commissioning day was so momentous that he proposed to … Barbara on the spot. And to those sailors standing where he did 65 years ago, he turned and said, "I wish I was sitting right out there with you," his voice cracking at the memory of being a 19 year old again, starting a life of adventure that ended up with him in the center of just about every major event of the late twentieth century. He talked about standing night watch on deck, in quiet solitude, and how he found comfort and inspiration in the starry midnight sky, "for it is in basking in the splendor of the stars that you will truly understand the majesty of creation and bear witness to the certain hand of God." He ended not by thanking the sponsors, or the shipbuilders, or even his family seated all around him on the deck. He ended by asking God in the heavens to keep each and every young soldier safe.

There were many navy traditions: the Captain talked about each sailor on the maiden voyage of a new ship as a "plank-owner," a reference to the days when sailors slept on deck, and each got to claim a certain plank as a bed. When ships were retired, many sailors took their plank home with them. And so when Doro Bush Koch issued the traditional command to these plank-owners to "bring this ship to life," the thousand or so of them all ran up the four gangplanks, circled the decks, and then scrambled into place to stand at attention facing the crowds. The band played "Anchors Aweigh" over and over and folks clapped to the beat.

I noticed that the higher they climbed up the levels of the ship—ten stories high, some of them—the windier it got. And the harder it blew, the tighter they held their white sailor caps with one hand, and secured their medals and ribbons to their chests with the other. Every one of them seemed to have as many medals and ribbons as the Joint Chiefs down on the dais. The Captain later explained they all were from the top of their classes, because competition was tough to get assigned to the *George H. W. Bush*. Once they were in place, everything was turned on—fog horns, whistles, bells, that alarm that sounds like "ah-hoooo-gah." You name it, they turned it on. Huge radar transmitters started spinning high above the bridge, and a jet fighter with engines running moved into place on the edge of the flight deck above the President's head. The anti-aircraft guns started up again. It was spectacular. Then came the part we all expected: four F-18's buzzed the crowd, low and loud. But wait, there's

Heroes don't only live in the past or just in the history books. They are all around us. They're shipbuilders. They're naval personnel.

President George H.W. Bush
January 2008

one more coming! We all squinted into the sun as a long plant followed. It was a WWII Avenger, the kind President Bush flew off the *"San Jac"* as he calls it. Every head turned from the torpedo bomber to 41 [former President Bush] at the podium. He threw his arms up in the air in surprise and delight, a human exclamation point. The Avenger headed toward the horizon to great cheers. Former President Bush handed a beautiful spyglass to the Captain, signifying the start of the first watch—which, once started, will never cease until the ship is retired. I don't think any of us will ever forget it.

What a day that was for all of us who had the opportunity to attend! As I said, that is a day that will linger in my mind for the rest of my life.

Final Thoughts

My goal many years ago was to travel and see the world, not knowing where my travels would take me. Little did I know that the world would be my oyster, as some would say, while making many friends along the way and reaching the highest levels of achievement in my flying career.

My father taught me at an early age that I could do anything that I wanted to do, be anything that I wanted to be—but to be willing to do whatever it takes to succeed by maintaining a positive attitude while not hurting anyone in the process.

It truly was an honor, privilege, and pleasure to serve. I feel at this stage of life that the best is yet to come, being a cancer survivor on the mend (recovering from my bout with prostate cancer and melanoma), knowing that I am a Christian, a happy grandfather, a patriot, and a man proud to be a citizen of the greatest country on the face of the earth: the United States of America.

WA